The
Caring Congregation
Ministry

Implementation Guide

Also Available

The Caring Congregation Ministry: Care Minister's Manual

Karen Lampe
Melissa Gepford

THE CARING
CONGREGATION
MINISTRY

IMPLEMENTATION GUIDE

Abingdon Press
Nashville

Contents

PART THREE: CARING FOR PEOPLE IN CRISIS

Lord, make me an instrument of your peace.
Where there is hatred, let me sow love;

Where there is injury, pardon. Where there is doubt, faith.
Where there is despair, hope. Where there is darkness, light.

And where there is sadness, joy.

O, Divine Master, grant that I may not so much seek to be consoled
as to console. To be understood as to understand. To be loved as to love.

For it is in giving that we receive. It is in pardoning that we are pardoned.
And it is in dying that we are born to eternal life.

—St. Francis of Assisi

Introduction

The ministry of congregational care is the heart of the church and should be carefully designed to help all of us get through challenging times. Congregational Care Ministers (CCMs) are key volunteers who work alongside their pastor to help provide Christlike care for the church family. This book is designed to train both pastors and volunteers so that together they can organize methods of care that are relevant to the needs of our current era.

You may wonder if you have the capacity to create, lead, and do this ministry. Much of your ability to care is born out of your own life story because whatever situations life has handed you, God can help you take those challenges, turn them inside out, and make good of them.

Everyone has a story about their life that involves challenge and choices. Just by being human means we will encounter complex situations. The times when I (Karen) grew the most were not easy.

In my early twenties, I found myself in a very abusive situation professionally that helped me understand salvation in a way like I never had. The depth of my pain and shame would have been helped by the healing power of the voices of the #MeToo movement. An amazing volunteer in our church helped me and my marriage survive. That was when I came to understand the power of the gospel message.

Through the challenges of life I found that my relationship with God grew exponentially, especially when I engaged with people of my faith. How we help one another get through difficult times requires a commitment to the healing ministries of our churches.

If you or a loved one has encountered fear or pain from cancer, a natural disaster, questions of sexual/gender identity, addiction, assault, depression, anxiety, or suicide of a loved one, you can experience your own resurrection that then prepares you to help others.

Rev. Melissa Gepford and I share a vision of the importance of congregational care that is fueled by the empowerment of the laity with the hope of expanding the ministry out into the community. Melissa and her husband have developed a CCM ministry in both a small church and now in a medium-size church. She is a pro at organizing for any size church and you will find her contributions to this text very helpful. Her own life story drives her devotion to this task.

How to Use This Book

This book is essential as you set up your care ministry and work consistently to develop the practical methods of care within your team. There are three parts to *The Caring Congregation Implementation Guide*.

Part 1 will give you details about how to organize your congregational care ministry by utilizing the Five Essentials. Each essential can be adjusted according to the size and needs of your church. Be patient as you evaluate and make needed changes.

Parts 2 and 3 will address relevant topics regarding care in very practical ways. Part 2 includes six chapters that serve as the six very important basic training sessions. Some of the focus areas consider issues such as boundaries, health, death, and pastoral listening.

Part 3 includes chapters that address specific needs your community may have, and this information can serve as continuing education training sessions. Critical issues we are currently facing such as addictions, depression and anxiety, suicides, as well as pandemic and other community crises induced by extreme weather or hate crimes are covered as we move forward to become a more relevant church in the twenty-first century.

The Care Minister's Manual is a **separate book** that serves as a training workbook and reference resource for each Congregational Care Minister.

The manual provides specific details and highlights for care, and teaches important techniques and methods for the CCM. These techniques and methods include talking points, lists of clarifying questions for the CCM, relevant scripture references, prayers to share during the course of care, and lists of other resources where CCMs can find additional information or help. The *Manual* is packed with tools to help pastors, other Congregational Care Ministry leaders, and CCMs develop their care ministry, keep it organized, and improve the ministry's capacity to care for the congregation and community. These tools include sample forms, templates, and checklists.

The most robust Congregational Care Ministries will begin with this book, the *Implementation Guide*, and then will conduct CCM training and ministry development utilizing the *Care Minister's Manual.*

Throughout this book you'll find callout boxes that emphasize best practices as well as personal stories. Also, at the end of each chapter there are segments to help you assess yourself and your community. Take time to evaluate and consider thoughtfully possible changes.

Care is such a vital ministry and sacred responsibility of the church. God has called us to walk alongside people during their most defining moments, and it is so important to have an effective system that works.

History of This Method of Care

This ministry of Congregational Care Ministers was started at the United Methodist Church of the Resurrection when we realized that our ministry could be so much more effective if we had a trained group of volunteers to help us with all of the caring ministries including hospital calls, support groups/classes, pastoral listening, and any other number of care needs. The CCMs became essential to our ministry, and now that ministry has been shared with churches throughout the United States. This model of care has been utilized and adapted for many different denominations and scales well to fit any size church.

Key Concepts

Four key concepts are emphasized throughout this book.

1. Embrace teamwork. There are no lone rangers in this ministry. Jesus had a team and we need teams to help us be the community of faith.

2. Trust that the Holy Spirit will be leading you in every aspect of your ministry. You are never alone and God will give you the tools you need for each situation.

3. Evaluate, evaluate, evaluate. I have had a sign in my office for many years that says, "Do not be afraid of change, be afraid of not changing." This sign has become a prayer for me as I invite others into the work of being a relevant church. Always be looking for new ways to keep your ministry effective and nimble.

4. In all things, pray first! Everything we do must be undergirded with prayerful discernment.

So with that in mind, let's pray:

Gracious, loving God, we come to you ever so grateful for all of the ways that our lives have been challenged because we know that in those times you have helped us to grow and become the people whom we are now. Give us courage to take every life experience that you might continue to use us to bring Christlike care to a hurting world. All this we pray in Christ's name. Amen.

Theology

Our theology, and how we express it, is foundational for the care ministries of our church. We have so many questions about how God works in the world:

o   Why does a loving God allow suffering?

o   What is the difference between healing and curing?

o   How can we facilitate the redemption process?

o   Do miracles still happen?

And the list goes on.

Yet this side of eternity, none of us fully understands how God's power works in and through us. As we study the life of Jesus, we understand that his healing ministry was central to who he was. Now he calls us to follow him and care for his lambs. Jesus challenges us in John 14:12 (NIV): "Very truly I tell you, whoever believes in me will do the works that I have been doing, and they will do even greater things than these." How we define our part in Jesus's healing ministry is integral to our theology. Thus we acknowledge our own need to grow in our faith through experience, reasoning, scripture, and tradition. This text will explore and develop our theological foundation regarding care so that God can use us as healers.

Organization

One of my mentors and teachers said to me, "Karen, you can have people read the books and teach them through a seminar, but they need to understand the basics of organizing the ministry." This statement is so very true.

As I have taught churches of all sizes across the country, it has become ever-more clear that there are five essential steps for organizing this ministry. These important ideas are addressed in detail throughout the text. As we begin, these five essentials will be explored in depth:

Five Essentials for Organizing Your Care Ministry

1.   Recruit and Equip. Choose and train the laity to become Congregational Care Ministers. Do not be afraid of empowering talented laity to use their gifts and graces. Training and deployment will take time, but it will be worth it! The church and

community will be blessed beyond measure and those who are trained will also find new purposes.

2. Identify Roles and Responsibilities. Choose key volunteers who will help the pastor organize, triage, and deploy the other volunteers.

3. Establish the Documentation System. Create confidential documentation systems that may be in both electronic and paper formats.

4. Evaluate. Evaluate the current care needs of your church and community. Do you have support ministries that are effective? For instance, for the past many years, there has been an epidemic of new addictions across the country. Who are the champions who could help you develop a recovery ministry? Dream big about how you will offer care not only for individuals but also for all the people in your community.

5. Build the Need. Communicate to your congregation your excitement about the CCMs and the importance of the healing ministries of the church.

This System Works Best with Three Primary Collaborative Roles

1. *Director of Congregational Care*—Typically, this role is embodied by a pastor; they are responsible for establishing and maintaining the Congregational Care Ministry. Responsibilities will include, but are not limited to, recruiting, training, and providing ongoing evaluation.

2. *Congregational Care Minister*—Laity become CCMs through a recruitment and application process. Once they are trained and commissioned, their responsibilities could include visitation, calls, one-on-one meetups, and care group leadership.

3. *Dispatcher*—The Dispatcher receives all prayer and visitation requests, calls, and submissions, and works with the Director

of Congregational Care to assign CCMs to each concern. For small to mid-sized churches, the Director of Congregational Care serves as the Dispatcher. For larger churches, you may need a Dispatcher for hospital calls, plus separate Dispatchers for elder care or requests for personal prayer.

How the Caring Congregation Ministry Model Works

Caring for people can get messy. We recognize that each person's concern or crisis is unique and will require wisdom in determining the next right step for them. As you work your way through this manual, you will encounter details and caveats to address possible scenarios for care. To avoid confusion or remaining caught in the weeds, we have outlined three general steps to provide care effectively as a congregation. We will further discuss each step in the following chapters.

1. *Intake and Dispatch*—Director and Dispatcher curate and assign each care request to a CCM (see the digital files for examples of prayer request cards and other useful resources for intake and dispatch).

2. *Follow Up*—CCMs receive their assignments weekly and follow up with the person requesting care.

3. *Documentation*—After each assigned follow-up, the CCM documents their interaction.

Now that you have a macro-view of the Congregational Care Ministry, our prayer is that you are even more convinced that this simple and streamlined, yet robust and versatile, system will bless you and your congregation. In part 1 of the text, we will explain how to set up your Congregational Care Ministry utilizing the Five Essentials.

Assessing Your Community

Get vulnerable for a few minutes and prayerfully ponder your life experiences. Consider some of your most important and transformative times in your life and how the church has been integral to your journey.

1. What is God calling you to do?

2. How will your story help the ministry to grow?

3. What are the resources you need to initiate this ministry?

4. Who can help you organize?

Part One

Establishing Your Congregational Care Ministry

Chapter One

First Essential:
Recruit and Equip

*Thank you, Creator God, for gifting your people with compassion and
enthusiasm to care for one another. We would ask that you help us encourage
one another in this journey, that surely we might offer the ministry of
Christlike healing to all who yearn for greater peace, new strength, and grace
beyond measure. All this we pray in Christ's name. Amen.*

I (Melissa) remember it like it was yesterday. My husband, Bill, was the
solo pastor at a small program-sized church in a town of five thousand.
I hadn't yet been commissioned as a deacon in The United Methodist
Church, but I worked on staff as the discipleship coordinator. It was a
busy week day in the office when we received a call at the church. One of
our members was in the hospital in Kansas City, just forty-five minutes
east of us. Bill hopped in the car and headed east.

Fifteen minutes down the road, his cell phone rang. Another congregant was in the ICU; it was urgent. Except she was in the hospital in
Lawrence, thirty minutes west of our little town.

Did I mention Bill was headed east?

It's a dilemma in which no pastor wants to find themselves: who
"gets" my care today? But that was the choice Bill had to make. That was
the day we (Bill and I, along with two other gifted souls from our church
whom I'll tell more about later) registered for The Caring Congregation

Seminar, hosted by Rev. Karen Lampe at United Methodist Church of the Resurrection.

I hope your moment wasn't as potent as ours, but I imagine something—an event, a dilemma, an honest mistake—led you to this resource. As the twenty-first-century American church stares down the realities of our country's declining physical and mental health, financial crises, and the inevitable "death tsunami" predicted by Rev. Dr. Lovett Weems, it's becoming crystal clear that a pastor-centric model of care just isn't sustainable. We can't do this alone—and we were never meant to!

The Case for Laity

Long before the advent of smartphones, social media, and twenty-four-hour accessibility, ministry leaders still had to take care of the flock. And somehow, they still had time to tend to their own spiritual growth, and take on hobbies like breeding dogs (Rev. John Russell), or writing entire books on health care (Rev. John Wesley).

The Apostle Paul, arguably the most effective church planter in history, planted churches and then left! How in the world was that model sustainable, and why did it flourish the way that it did?

All human beings have certain gifts, skills, and abilities—but not by accident. God gave us these gifts and has called each of us to use them to be a blessing to the world. Paul talks about the church working like a body in 1 Corinthians 12:12-18:

> Christ is just like the human body—a body is a unit and has many parts; and all the parts of the body are one body, even though there are many. We were all baptized by one Spirit into one body, whether Jew or Greek, or slave or free, and we all were given one Spirit to drink. Certainly the body isn't one part but many. If the foot says, "I'm not part of the body because I'm not a hand," does that mean it's not part of the body? If the ear says, "I'm not part of the body because I'm not an eye," does that mean it's not part of the body? If the whole body were an eye, what would happen to the hearing? And if the whole body were an ear, what would happen to the sense of smell? But as it is, God has placed each one of the parts in the body just like he wanted.

In my time serving on the Congregational Excellence team for the Great Plains Annual Conference, I've learned that the key ingredient for an excellent congregation is excellent laity—people who are convinced of their call to ministry in every vocation, utilizing their God-given gifts for the sake of making disciples of Jesus for the transformation of the world.

Pastors, it's time to get out of the way. Your people have been gifted by God—some of them to care for others—and when we take the reins for ourselves, we deny people opportunities to be who they were called to be.

The First Class

The drive from the Caring Congregation Seminar to our bedroom community was forty-five minutes. After two days of soaking up all we could at the seminar, you would think we'd have been exhausted. Not so! On the way home, our team—comprising my husband; Carissa, our youth group leader; Alice, a gifted layperson; and myself—spent the entire forty-five minutes brainstorming, tailoring, and beginning the first and most vital step to a successful Congregational Care Ministry: identifying that first class of CCMs.

The Congregational Care Minister is the foundation of the ministry. Without ministers, the system collapses, which is why it is so vital, especially in the early stages, to choose the right people with the right dispositions to serve. The following section will help you identify qualities in an ideal care minister.

The Ideal Care Minister

The Congregational Care Ministry is modeled after Jesus, who healed the sick, cared for the poor, and had compassion on those who suffered physically, mentally, spiritually, and systemically. Upon reading the Gospels, we encounter the Wounded Healer willing to touch the untouchables, interact with those on the margins of society, and deliver people from all sorts of ailments with compassion, dignity, and empathy. This is the example we follow as disciples of Christ and as care ministers.

Easier said than done, right? I know I don't live up to that standard all the time, and the beauty of the good news is that there's grace when we don't emulate Jesus as well as we would like to. And the beauty of the Congregational Care Ministry model is that, while we strive to embody Jesus's example, we also follow a long and historical tradition of caring for others in our midst. Care didn't stop with Jesus.

Before Jesus was arrested and crucified, he sat at a table with his closest companions. He got up, took his outer garments off, wrapped himself in a towel, and began washing the disciples' feet. It was a shocking display of servanthood—one the disciples didn't quite understand. Jesus explained his entire ministry in that subversive act: he was the leader of a movement threatening to topple the empire, yet he took on the work of a servant. The way of Jesus is servant leadership, and he calls us to the same.

That same night, Jesus commanded the disciples to love one another. It seems obvious, but with a group like the disciples—full of zealots and tax collectors and Roman collaborators—Jesus needed to say it out loud one more time. Because the only way people will know we follow Jesus is if we love one another. That's it. The way we love one another, the way we care for one another—that's the model we strive for with the Congregational Care Ministry.

After Jesus ascended to heaven, the disciples were left to continue his ministry on earth. As the movement grew, it became clear that they needed to organize by defining roles and responsibilities. Acts 6 tells us that the needs of some of the most vulnerable people in their midst were being neglected, so the disciples chose a core group of seven *diakonia*, from which we derive the word *deacon*, to provide care and concern for those who needed it.

In the New Testament, *diakonia* was the ministry of service, aid, and support. The word began as a word to describe a person who waits on tables, then expanded to someone who cared for all household needs, and eventually came to mean general service. It naturally implies a level of personal subjugation to another, putting a person's needs above their own.

Deacons in the early church were women and men who assisted in liturgical logistics; proclamation of the word and Christian mission; and general ministry in the church, which included a variety of actions. As the role of the *diakonos* developed, it became one in which servant leaders attended to public worship, the care of the poor, and administration.

An early church collection of treatises known as the Apostolic Constitutions prescribes that deacons are to visit "all those who stand in need of visitation,"[1] and Cyprian of Carthage called on those in ministry to "always pray for one another" and to "relieve burdens and afflictions by mutual love."[2]

Ministry leaders, as you begin implementing the first essential, consider laypeople who embody servant leadership, prayer, and mutual love, care, and concern. Who comes to mind? Jot down their names. Let your list be as short or long as you are led, then pray over your potential CCMs.

On the way home from the seminar, we had so much fun brainstorming all the folks in our midst who embodied such admirable and Christlike qualities that we found our list was actually too long! Our average worship attendance was around 175, so we only needed five CCMs in addition to our pastoral staff. We didn't need as many people as we had listed, so we began narrowing down, utilizing the criteria provided in *The Caring Congregation Training Manual and Resource Guide*:

1. Active member who has established a deep connection to the church.

2. Regular worship attendance.

3. Scriptural and theological foundation, and a willingness to learn.

4. Knowledge and study of scripture to provide a foundation for care ministry.

5. Active pursuit of growth in the Christian life through participation in a small group or some other form of Christian discipleship.

6. Deeply committed Christian who lives out a life of faith through acts of piety (love of God) and mercy (love of neighbor).

7. Giving financially in proportion to their income with the tithe being the goal.

8. Safe gatherings or other types of certification to assure their understanding of boundaries. Each church needs to decide what type of certification will be required.

9. Expected to commit to at least three hours per week to this ministry.[3]

We found that some on our list embodied all of these qualities, while others weren't as regular in their worship attendance as we'd have liked our CCMs to be. A couple others would have been a great fit, but we already knew how busy their schedules were, and we knew they wouldn't be able to commit the amount of time each week we knew we needed. After a time of discernment, we had identified our five CCMs we wanted for our first class, and we began recruiting.

Ministry leaders, take a look at your list of possible CCMs again. Identify how many you'd like in your first class of CCMs, and take a look at the criteria provided. Who stands out now?

Recruiting Your CCMs

Once you have narrowed your list down to the ones you believe would be a great first class of CCMs, it's time to recruit! Here are a few tips for effective CCM recruitment:

1. Pray, pray, pray. Pray for the church, the ministry, the people who have been called to care for others, and those who will be receiving care on behalf of the congregation. Ask God to give you eyes to see gifts in those who provide care well.

2. Be picky and practice discernment. Don't be OK with "any warm body" who will say yes to your begging. We don't work out of a scarcity mentality!

3. Face-to-face invitation to apply. Seek out individuals you've intentionally identified as possible CCMs. Phone calls, emails, texts, and pulpit/bulletin announcements certainly are helpful, but be careful with how you extend the invitation. Make it clear that there is an application process that will discern if being a CCM is a good fit. This is an invitation, not an ask, favor, or plea. Invite applicants to join you in sharing God's care and concern to the congregation and community.

Notice that the third point is an invitation to *apply*. Even if you already have a good idea of who should make up your core leadership team and subsequent CCMs, ask these persons to fill out an application. This is a vital step as the ministry continues to grow and more and more people are interested in serving as a CCM.

You may receive some pushback and even criticism for this, since many churches function in a "first come, first served" or "sign up to serve" mentality. For some ministries of the church, that model is great! We want to allow opportunities for all people to serve in some capacity at the church. The Congregational Care Ministry is not one of those opportunities. CCMs will be deployed on behalf of the church to provide care to people facing some of their darkest, most confusing times in their lives, and it is imperative to vet and train those who will share in these moments.

Determine your selection process ahead of time. We suggest a two-phase process:

1. Each person is asked to fill out an application, which asks for a spiritual biography.

2. Following the application submission, interviews are conducted with a pastor and staff member.

Consider the following interview questions:

1. What are two or three things in your life/faith story that are defining moments for you?

2. Tell me about how worship plays a role in your life.

3. What has been your discipleship journey so far?

4. In what ways have you practiced Christian service?

5. Tell me about any class or Bible studies you've participated in.

6. Why do you want to be a CCM? What does a life totally surrendered to God mean to you?

7. What does your daily practice of the spiritual disciplines look like? How do you explain grace? What is your faith autobiography?

8. When have you had a challenging experience in your life? What did you do? Who was involved? How did you handle it? From whom did you seek help?

9. Imagine you are in a one-on-one scenario, giving care. Who benefits? Where is God in this?

The interviewer informs the applicant that someone will call soon. Close by praying with the applicant. After the interview, debrief with your interview team, share any notes you take, and make decisions.

Not every member of your congregation will have the gifts and skills necessary to fill this role of caring for the congregation. In these cases, we try to direct people to other possibilities for volunteering where their unique gifts can best be used. Trust your gut and the collective experience of others. It is far better to redirect applicants to another area of ministry early in the discernment process rather than have a difficult conversation later about possible other places to serve. Some questions to consider as you practice discernment:

1. Are they healed from past wounds?

2. Do they need more time or experience to study? If so, invite them to apply again in the future.

3. Would there be a better fit for their gifts in a different ministry area?

Equipping Your CCMs

Once your CCMs have said yes, it's crucial to equip them well. CCMs will be partnering with pastors to offer some of the care previously done only by a pastor, so it is important that these persons have basic theological and biblical training. We suggest equipping your CCMs with theological and biblical training through an intensive study like Disciple Bible Study, Christian Believer, or a similar resource.

It is also imperative to train your CCMs in the logistics and practices of the Congregational Care Ministry model. We invite you to utilize parts 2 and 3 of this book as a script for training the basics. These training modules work best when each CCM receives the companion resource, *The Caring Congregation Ministry: Care Minister's Manual.*

Training can be done over the course of a weekend, seminar-style. It can also be broken into one module per week over the course of a couple of months. The COVID-19 pandemic forced us all to reimagine former ways of connecting and learning, and we encourage you to continue offering digital options for accessible training. Decide what works best for your context and your CCMs. Once you have established the model for training, determine your dates. If other churches in the area or in your network are also implementing the Congregational Care Ministry, consider hosting a training together to share resources and teaching responsibilities. Secure a room large enough to accommodate your CCMs with round tables and chairs of no more than eight people at each table. If you are hosting a seminar-style weekend, consider kicking off your event with a worship service and closing with the commissioning service provided to you in chapter 5. Be sure to purchase a copy of the *Care Minister's Manual* for each participant, along with any other commissioning gifts, which could include a Bible, anointing vials, congregational care card sets (can be purchased at https://thewell.cor.org/), official CCM name tags with the church's logo, and official CCM business cards and stationery with the church's logo (these come in handy during visits, especially in nursing facilities or hospitals, to leave a note if the person is sleeping when a CCM arrives or is unable to remember the visit).

Continuing Education

Once your CCMs have completed the basic training modules, we encourage you to regularly provide continuing education opportunities for your CCMs. The chapters in part 3 of this book serve as some jumping-off points as you consider offering continuing education. It is up to you to determine what "regular" looks like in your context. For some churches, quarterly meetings are sufficient and helpful; other churches host weekly meetings to unpack, share insights, and bring case studies to the group. Possible topics for continuing education could include member assistance, medical information, caring for the frail, hospice care, information technology, ministry to people with dementia and their families, self-care, development of a recovery ministry, and mental health ministry. The possibilities are endless!

Assessing Your Community

In this chapter, you have learned that the first essential to building your Congregational Care Ministry is to recruit and equip your Congregational Care Ministers. As you begin implementing the first essential, take some time to reflect on the following questions and ideas.

1. What does an ideal Congregational Care Minister look like in your context?

2. Brainstorm a list of laity who exhibit gifts that align with those of a CCM.

3. Develop a plan for recruiting your first class of CCMs.

Chapter Two

Second Essential: Identify Roles and Responsibilities

Gracious Loving God, we are grateful that you have given each of us unique gifts and experiences that have made us able to serve you in our individual ways. We lift up our hearts to you that we might receive your divine seed that encourages us to more fully devote ourselves to your healing ministry. Bless each one with the belief that they are able to bid your calling in Christ's name. Amen.

My husband, Bill, and I (Melissa) registered for the Caring Congregation Seminar knowing that it couldn't be only our initiative. For the sake of the ministry in our church that had around 180 in worship on a Sunday, we needed to identify some laity to come alongside us and really build our Congregational Care Ministry from the ground up. The reality was, there were quite a few people who were already caring for our congregation; all we needed to do was give them the tools and training to make it "official." We invited two amazing women to join us for the seminar: Alice and Carissa.

Carissa was in her late twenties, loud and colorful. She led our youth group, had a toddler, and was systematically working on finishing her sleeve tattoo. She was a licensed social worker with experience in group homes for children in unfortunate circumstances. She had her own struggles and past experiences that formed her into a compassionate yet fiery advocate for the underdog and the misunderstood. Carissa knew anxiety and depression deep within her soul, so when someone needed prayer and a listening ear as they navigated through anxiety or family problems that required intervention, Carissa was there for them.

Alice was warm, inviting, and embodied a kind of grace and hospitality that was unique to her being. She also had been a nurse, experienced a painful divorce, and beat cancer three times. Who do you think we sent to care for those who were caught in relationship problems or undergoing cancer treatment? Of course it was Alice.

These two women couldn't be more different. Yet something bound them together. It was their love for Jesus and for people, their compassion and concern for the hurting, their drive and desire to bring light into the dark nights of the soul. They both relied on their past experiences to care for others in their own ways, and because of their differences, our ministry was able to care for more people with different types of concerns and struggles.

Because of Alice's experiences with cancer, she was able to care for a beloved member who had just been diagnosed with a brain tumor. Because of Carissa's experience with underprivileged children, she was the go-to CCM for families that struggled to make ends meet. As we spent more time together caring for our congregation, we began to identify specific niches, roles, and responsibilities that enabled us to expand our impact as a caring congregation.

Three Primary Roles

The Congregational Care Ministry system works best with three primary collaborative roles:

1. *Director of Congregational Care.* Typically, this role is embodied by a pastor. They are responsible for establishing and maintaining the Congregational Care Ministry. Responsibilities will include, but are not limited to, recruiting, training, providing ongoing evaluation, and caring for the CCMs. Gifts will include, but are not limited to, vision-casting, organization, care, system-building, and discernment.

2. *Congregational Care Minister.* Laity become CCMs through a recruitment and application process. Once they are trained and commissioned, their responsibilities could include visitation, calls, one-on-one meetups, and care group leadership. Gifts will include, but are not limited to, compassion, empathy, interpersonal warmth, and the ability to define and stick to personal boundaries.

3. *Dispatcher.* The Dispatcher receives all prayer and visitation requests, calls, and submissions, and works with the Director of Congregational Care to assign CCMs to each concern. Call and connect with each CCM every week to assign new duties and hear how assignments are going. For small to mid-sized churches, the Director of Congregational Care may serve as the Dispatcher. For larger churches, you may need a Dispatcher for hospital calls, plus separate Dispatchers for elder care or requests for personal prayer. Gifts will include, but are not limited to, organization, communication, technology skills, discernment.

All three roles rely upon one another: The Director sets up the model and works with the Dispatcher to assign CCMs on an ongoing basis. The Dispatcher connects with CCMs weekly to get feedback and continue assignments, sharing that information with the Director. The CCMs receive care from the Director as they care for others, assignments from the Dispatcher, and support from one another.

These three roles are crucial for the Congregational Care Ministry model, but you may find that, in your context, additional roles are appropriate. If your model already includes a number of teams like prayer teams, card-making groups, funeral meal teams, and so forth, you might identify leaders of each group who serve as the core leadership of the Congregational Care Ministry so that all groups collaborate to provide the best care possible. In larger contexts, assistants may help with some of the logistical pieces. In even larger contexts with multiple pastors, you might create a tiered approach to care in which specific worship services have one main pastor with a team of CCMs. This model is nimble enough to expand or be tailored down to your needs.

During my time as a consultant, I have encountered churches establishing their Congregational Care Ministries from scratch. Other times, I've worked with ministry leaders to organize their already-existing care ministry under the umbrella of congregational care. In these instances, I worked with individuals to tailor it to fit their needs. A few tweaks were necessary, but in a system with laity already providing care, it's a matter of organization and documentation rather than building from scratch. Establishing the congregational care model doesn't mean you have to shut down other care ministries that already exist; it simply means that the church already has a DNA of lay care. Use that momentum and build upon it! That being said, this may also be a good time to help your team evaluate what is working well and what may be needed to transition.

In all of my consultation calls, the most consistent work includes identifying and clarifying each CCM's roles and responsibilities. In a smaller system, there may be less flexibility to "specialize." The smaller the church, the more likely that each CCM will take on multiple roles and responsibilities. The larger the ministry grows, the more likely a CCM will specialize into a niche of care.

Specialized Care

As previously stated, each CCM has their own lived experiences that make them uniquely situated to care for people with specific circumstances. Some people are relational and are quite capable of making hospital visits, telephone calls, or sitting with people who need encouragement and prayer. Some CCMs have great administrative skills and provide amazing support help. Some CCMs may be professionally adept with finances, counseling, or medicine. It is significantly more meaningful to receive care and prayer from someone who has had similar experiences as you. Dispatchers and Directors must know their CCMs well enough to know who might be able to best care for whom. This takes time and intentionality. Ministry leaders, spend time with your CCMs, asking them questions about their lives, experiences, passions, and what makes them tick. When you train your CCMs, make it a point to get to know them during breaks, in between sessions, and beyond.

In one local church appointment, I hosted a dinner party for our CCMs. After getting to know them on a more personal level, I felt better equipped to make discerning calls when it came to assigning CCMs to specific prayer and care requests. Dale had been burned by the church before. He experienced a faith leader at their worst, and because of that, he wrestled with doubt and how prayer "works." So when someone needed care but felt resistant to a pastor and the religious platitudes that seem like a cliché during a faith crisis, Dale was able to care for them in a way that a pastor never could.

Brittany was a teacher, who had spent her entire career in the community. She was soft-spoken, a calm yet unwavering presence to those for whom she cared. So when we found out that Dante, who needed care during a hospitalization, was Brittany's student so many years before, we sent Brittany to pray with him.

Chandler was every man's man. He enjoyed golf, shooting the breeze, and painting houses. He had the uncanny ability to put anyone at ease with his easygoing attitude and lighthearted jokes. Chandler's presence calmed those with anxiety and depression.

Jasmyn was in high school when she was commissioned. Her life stage alone allowed her to care for young people in a way no adult could. She cared deeply for her peers by spending time with them, baking goodies for them, and providing a listening ear with the same perspective as those for whom she cared.

You get the picture: each person brings their own gifts and experiences to the table, which uniquely positions them to care for others. This is why it is so vital to continue to get to know your CCMs while assigning them specific roles and responsibilities.

Launch Team

In my first church to implement the Congregational Care Ministry model, we identified our launch team early on with the intentions of growing into a specialized care model. There already had been some of that

DNA in our congregation; a pair of two women had been visiting nursing facilities for years. Thankfully, they continued their work so that we could focus on launching additional care for the community. Eventually, this already-existing ministry was brought under the umbrella of congregational care, further expanding the "niche care" idea. They continued their regular visits as CCMs, while the others focused on calls and other responsibilities.

Our launch team included:

o   a Director of Congregational Care, who also functioned as the Dispatcher;

o   a senior pastor, who functionally served as a specialist CCM, caring for all funerals and critical care needs; and

o   three Congregational Care Ministers, who served as generalists at first. The more specific the prayer requests became, the more they grew into specialized care.

Your context likely differs from my experience, so you may find that you need a different structure for your launch team. Regardless of structure or number of people, your launch team is a crucial part of establishing a sustainable and flourishing Congregational Care Ministry.

Assessing Your Community

This chapter discusses the three primary roles and responsibilities of the Congregational Care Ministry model and explains how the roles can become more specialized over time, according to each CCM's gifts and experiences. As you begin implementing the second essential, take some time to reflect on the following questions.

1.   You've identified your CCMs; now, which of the three roles might they each fit into?

2.   Are there additional roles necessary in your context?

3.   What might that look like?

4.   How will all of the roles collaborate to provide the best care possible?

Chapter Three

Third Essential: Establish the Documentation System

Everything should be done with dignity and in proper order.

—1 Corinthians 14:40

At the Caring Congregation Seminar some years ago, our team of four leaned in. We learned the theology, the practicalities, the logistics—all of it. I took copious amounts of notes, scribbling in the margins of my workbook. Our team was fired up; during the seminar breaks, we stood around the coffee station, wide-eyed with hope for the future.

Our final session before closing worship was all about documentation. This session answered the question I had been asking since day one: This information is great—but how do we organize it? I was most concerned with keeping good records, staying organized, and making this system work for our situation. The session leader introduced the paperwork and talked about an organizational piece of software called Arena that helped them keep track of everything. It seemed like a dream, but we didn't have the budget, or the need, to replicate their model. How could we tailor a program built for a megachurch like Church of the Resurrection to fit our church that had 180 in worship on any given Sunday? This chapter is all about establishing a documentation system that works for your setting.

The Case for Records

For every church, there is a history of the care and shepherding of the people. Usually, however, that history lies in the hearts and minds of the pastors who have served the church and the congregation. In order to give excellent care, it is imperative to build a recorded history. This history will help the caregivers remember what has been offered and what might still be in order for care. Missteps can be avoided, and good decisions are more likely to be made to achieve the best care.

Records help maintain institutional and personal memory and provide a transition when pastors change, leave, or are not available. They help avoid "time flies" problems and address claims that you didn't give care to a congregant. Documenting conversations relieves congregants of the pain of retelling a traumatic story repeatedly, and it reminds people that they are cared for and remembered.

In the introduction, we outlined the three general steps to providing care effectively as a congregation: intake and dispatch, follow up, and documentation. In this chapter, we will discuss the logistical side of each step. More of the practical and theological details for "follow up" are covered in parts 2 and 3 of this book.

Intake and Dispatch

Developing a clear and concise pathway for intake and dispatch can be tedious work. You should be able to articulate in one sentence to an elementary-aged child how to request care at your church, while also taking into consideration multiple layers of strategic pieces. Know who receives all requests behind the scenes, how CCMs receive their assignments, and develop a predictable and reliable weekly flow to guarantee quality care on behalf of your church.

Often, churches rely on word of mouth, and sometimes, congregants come to expect that pastors just know when someone needs care. Without prayer request cards, a call to the office, or at least an email, how can we know? I invite you to inventory your intake system and brainstorm ways to make requesting prayer as accessible as possible. Consider stocking your sanctuary with prayer request cards, and adding a digital way to request prayer and care on your church's website and very specific locations on social media pages, like direct messaging or a button that takes someone to your website. Designate a CCM with tech and organizational skills to curate all of these requests each week. In many cases, an office staff person may be the point person for this kind of work. That can also be helpful, since calls to the church requesting care are common. Design a system that flows smoothly when curating and communicating all care requests to the Dispatcher. In its most basic form, that could be a shared spreadsheet with pastors and CCMs.

Publicizing Prayer Requests

Prayer requests are so important to the congregation, and many local churches make their prayer requests public in the bulletin or worship slides on Sunday morning. Whether a person has a new baby, faces a life-threatening disease, or sends a loved one off to college, people want to enlist their community of faith to pray with them. It is wise to keep this list fresh and up-to-date with no one on the list for more than two weeks. If there are long-term prayer concerns, consider making a list that is available online. Such lists might include military support and long-term health concerns.

Many congregations continue to lift prayer requests up by name during the worship service. A word of caution: as more and more worship services are livestreamed, it is absolutely crucial to consider how you will guarantee confidentiality in the digital age. Do not share names and details of a prayer request without permission from the one for whom you are offering prayer. Confidentiality is always a high priority as the church seeks to be highly sensitive to the needs of the faith family and the community.

Each church should evaluate exactly how they best communicate the prayer requests of their community. One essential method is to create a covenant prayer team and online prayer lists for people in the military and people with chronic illnesses. The covenant prayer team would receive lists of prayer requests throughout the week. Only the first name would be given to this team and a general description of what is requested for prayer, which keeps daily prayers flowing throughout the congregation.

How Prayer Request Cards Work

A tried and true method for collecting prayer requests is to make prayer request cards available during worship. Attendees are encouraged to write their requests during the service and drop them into the offering plates. People who worship online are also invited to submit their requests on a digital form accessible on the website and on any social media platforms.

Weekly, the Director and Dispatcher curate and assign each care request to a CCM. Collect prayer request cards and any other forms of care requests your church utilizes. Enter the requests into one location. Google Sheets provides a simple format to record contacts. Assign a CCM to each request, then contact the CCMs with their new assignments for the week (email is an efficient way to communicate with your CCMs). After CCMs have followed up with their assignments, they should document the interactions with the care recipients. The following weekly flow has proven to be predictable and efficient:

- o Monday: Dispatcher works with the administrative assistant to curate all prayer and care requests. Dispatcher meets with the Director of Congregational Care to assign CCMs. Dispatcher sends email to CCMs with assignments for the week.

- o Tuesday—Sunday: CCMs read and acknowledge their assignments for the week. They make care calls and visits then document their interactions.

- o If non-emergent requests for care come midweek, via phone or online, they are held until the following Monday's curation day. If emergency requests for care come midweek, the Dispatcher and Director discern whether to assign a CCM or a pastor for care. The nature of the emergency determines this decision. If your church has a prayer team, consider how to handle prayer requests midweek.

Hospital Care Systems

It is crucial for a church to keep track of hospitalizations in order to provide adequate care for those hospitalized and their families. Here are a few of the systems a church could easily utilize:

Hospital Notebook (paper or digital)

o   Full legal name of patient

o   Names of family members or friends who will be there during hospitalization

o   Reason for hospitalization

o   Location of hospital and time of admission

o   If surgery is scheduled, when the person will arrive and the time of the surgery

o   Who will visit from church?

o   How often will visits be made?

Hospital Board in Church Office

This is much the same information as contained in the hospital note-book. The notebook, however, contains more information. The hospital board gives minimal information to be used by staff and CCMs who are keeping track of people in the hospital.

o   Use a dry-erase board, chalkboard, bulletin board, or a card file that can be kept in a confidential area of the congregational care offices.

o   Fill the board with information about the hospitalization:

   –   Legal first and last name of person hospitalized

   –   Name of hospital and room number

- Reason for hospitalization (If surgery is scheduled, identify the type and time of surgery and anticipated length of surgery, if known).
- Pastor or CCM assigned to visit and dates of visit

Follow Up

At least once a week, CCMs should receive their assignments for care with the expectation that they follow up with the assignment in a timely manner. It is helpful for CCMs to receive guidance on the best way to follow up with a particular assignment—for some, a phone call is sufficient, but for others, a face-to-face interaction is preferable. In cases of illness, you may even choose to host a video chat via Zoom, Google Calls, FaceTime, or another platform. Regardless, a simple phone call is the first step in following up. CCMs must have the care requesters' phone numbers available to them so that they do not have to spend time hunting down contact information.

Often, prayer request cards include a prayer for a person, requested by someone else. People pray for their friends, family, and loved ones, and it is natural to request prayer from the church. However, because we cannot know if that person has been given permission to share what they have written on a card, CCMs should follow up with the person who has requested prayer (the requester), *not* the person for whom they've requested prayer. For instance, if Matt writes a prayer request for his mother's health (who may or may not be a member), do not call the mother; rather you start with a call to Matt. Sometimes people will request on the card that the church call the mother or the friend or neighbor, but always call the requester to see if the party who is most affected would want us to reach out. Encourage the requester to reach out on behalf of the church. Then the CCM could ask if the person would like the church to participate in their care.

I learned this the difficult way when a CCM in my first church called to pray with a woman struggling with illness, and it turned out that the woman had shared her illness confidentially with someone else! It feels counterintuitive to follow up with the one requesting prayer, but we must do so in order to do no harm. Sometimes, though, it *is* appropriate to call the one for whom prayer has been requested—it may be a well-known prayer request in the church or community, or the requester has secured permission to share. Often, I have encountered CCMs unsure about whom to call in order to provide the best care possible, so I created a flowchart to help them discern.

CCM DOCUMENTATION

CCM checks email to find prayer/care assignments for the week on the shared spreadsheet.
Do you see your name for an assignment?

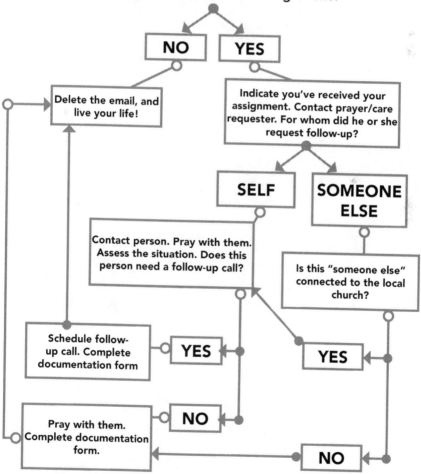

Documentation

Immediately following a care conversation, the CCM should document the most important information, which includes:

o name of congregant,

o date when care was given,

o reason for care,

o type of visit (phone, in person, etc.),

o CCM responsible,

o pastor responsible,

o last time the person was contacted,

o follow-up date, if needed, and

o other notes.

This information can be stored in a shared drive, on paper, or on some other platform. Regardless of the mode, this information should be kept in a safe place for confidential purposes, while also being accessible to, at least, the Director of Congregational Care. We do this for accountability and information sharing, should another CCM be providing care for that person in another CCM's absence.

A word on confidentiality: the trust that people give to you as pastors and CCMs can never be overlooked. You must be vigilant in this regard. To this end, set guidelines on the type of information that should be kept under lock and key, accessible to the pastor only. If the documents are digital, be sure they are either password protected, require a church-issued email address, or both.

Helpful Tools

The size of your congregation will dictate your dispatch and documentation system and the tools used to build it. For larger churches, programs like Shelby or Arena will be necessary in order to store all information.

Mid-sized churches might consider monday.com, a platform that creates Gantt charts, flowcharts, organization charts, and surveys.

For small to mid-sized congregations, there are free tools just a click away. As technology progresses, it is likely that new platforms will emerge with features appropriate to the Congregational Care Ministry documentation system. I invite you to continue to be on the lookout for the best way to document the care at your church.

Google Drive has proven to be a very reliable platform to build and store a documentation system. Google Drive is a free file storage and synchronization service that allows multiple users to view and edit documents, when shared with them. Google Drive includes a suite of applications that will enable you to work efficiently and effectively. We mostly used Google Sheets (a shareable and collaborative spreadsheet) for intake and dispatch, Gmail (email platform) to share information and assignments with CCMs, and Forms (an easy survey) for documentation following a care call or visit. To get the best out of your Google Drive experience, follow these guidelines:

Create a Google Account for the Church.

This will serve as the primary account to communicate with CCMs through Gmail and to store all prayer requests and documentation in your Google Drive. If you already have a personal Google account, I encourage you to create one solely for the church's care ministry. I learned this the hard way when I left a church and accidentally deleted all their care files to clear up some space in my own personal account!

Request That Every CCM Create a Personal Google Account.

If each CCM already has one, it is just fine to use those. We ask that every CCM has a Google account to ensure a higher level of confidentiality. It also creates a sense of continuity for the ministry, especially as email addresses are shared with those for whom they are caring.

Build a Document for Curating All Prayer and Care Requests.

This document will also be the dispatch document that you share with your CCMs. Naming it "Confidential Care Dispatch" may be helpful. It communicates that sensitive nature of the information, so that it is not shared with others outside of the Congregational Care Ministry. It also communicates to CCMs that this document includes their assignments for the week. You will not need to create multiple documents. Keep adding requests to this initial document, and archive the requests that have already been handled by moving them to a separate tab. This document should include the following columns: Date, Prayer Request, Requested By, Requester's Contact Information, CCM Assignment, and Additional Notes.

Documents work best if they each have clear titles around the level of care. You may want to consider adding a column that identifies the level of care needed.

- o Critical care (physical and mental)
  - – hospitalization
  - – hospice
  - – cancer, chemotherapy, radiation treatments
  - – mental illness, including suicide attempt or admittance into a psychiatric facility
- o Continued care
  - – cancer in remission
  - – recovery from surgery
  - – rehabilitation or post-operation
  - – relationship problems
  - – problems managing stress
  - – spiritual issues and questions
  - – mental health problems (bipolar disorder, anxiety, depression, anger, addictions, obsessive-compulsive disorder)
- o Long-term care
  - – homebound

- – resident of care center (coordinate with pastor)
- – grief of family member
- – long-term financial problems, unemployment, chronic illness/pain
- o Care by another team
  - – critical relationships (counselor)
  - – financial problems (financial advisor)
  - – other pastors
- o Archived
  - – no further action is required
  - – congregant may transition back to care lists at any given time
  - – archives maintained for one year

Build a Form for Care Documentation.

CCMs should use this after every care call or visit. Questions should include name of care recipient, name of CCM, date of care, type of visit, details of visit, follow-up notes (important dates coming up, next visit, hospital changes, discussion topics, etc.).

Generate a Sheet from Care Documentation Responses.

As CCMs utilize the Care Documentation Form, those responses can then be generated into a document. Once the document is generated, responses automatically update into the same document that can be shared with all CCMs, which is beneficial since the document provides brief but clear information and allows caregivers to sort by name, follow-up date, CCM assigned to care, and so on.

Each Week, Send an Email with Three Attachments.

Include a greeting, thanking CCMs for their work, then include (1) Confidential Care Dispatch Document; (2) Care Documentation Form;

and (3) Care Documentation Responses. Every week, I sent virtually the same email, similar to this example:

Dear CCMs,

Thank you so much for providing such wonderful care on behalf of the church! You are making a huge impact on the lives around you and in our community. Please see the attached Confidential Care Dispatch Document to view your new assignments for the week. Once you have followed up with your assignments, be sure to document your interactions on the Care Documentation Form. If you would like to look back on past documentation, feel free to look at the Care Documentation Responses Document. It may give you some reminders concerning someone you've been caring for a while.

I hope you have a wonderful week. Please do not hesitate to reach out if you have any questions or concerns!

Paper in the Digital Age

It may be the case that some of your CCMs are not comfortable utilizing the types of technology previously mentioned. Digital documentation should never be the reason a person chooses not to serve as a CCM. While digital documentation and communication are most effective and efficient, please keep in mind that not every CCM will possess the skills or hardware to function on a platform that requires computer or smartphone capability. Consider how you might incorporate a paper documentation option for those who become anxious when operating digitally. Perhaps they turn in paper copies of documentation and an assistant logs them into the digital storage system.

Assessing Your Community

No matter your church's size or budget, you have tools at your fingertips to create and sustain an organized system of care that takes seriously confidentiality, efficiency, and compassion, all in one. In this chapter, we outlined how to establish your documentation system. Now, it's your turn to do it! You should be able to clearly articulate your documentation system with your CCMs during training so that they feel equipped and empowered to care for the congregation. Ideally, this system is communicated to your CCMs after they receive theological and practical training and prior to their commissioning. Consider the following questions to guide your work:

Intake and Dispatch

o Articulate in one sentence how congregants can request care at your church.

o Who receives those requests, and what happens next?

o How do CCMs know what their assignments for the week are?

o Develop a predictable weekly flow for CCMs to guarantee care.

Follow Up

o What are the ways that CCMs will follow up?

o What tools will you offer to CCMs so that they feel well equipped to discern how to handle all types of prayer and care requests?

Documentation

o How will we guarantee confidentiality with documentation?

o Consider usability for CCMs when documenting; what might work best for them?

o How will all information be stored?

Discerning Which Tools to Utilize

o How many separate calls/visits per week does your care team collectively implement?

o How familiar are your CCMs with new technology? How adaptive can they be?

o How much storage do you need to maintain clear records of care?

Chapter Four

Fourth Essential: Evaluate

Great God of new visions, we come to you believing that your Holy Spirit is guiding us as we seek new life in your church. Inspire and call us to step out by faith into this season of perpetual creativity and transition. Let us not grow weary or fearful. Rather, pour within us new energy and enthusiasm as we seek to be co-creators with you. All this in Christ's name. Amen.

(Melissa) don't know about you, but my favorite jeans have a little *give* to them. They're the right length for my short frame, and they stretch just the right amount in the right places for my build. But around week twenty of my pregnancy, they stopped stretching—while I kept growing!

My husband, on the other hand, has a different kind of favorite jeans. They don't stretch at all. In fact, they shrink! When he needs a new pair of jeans, he purchases the Levi's 501 Original Shrink-to-Fit Men's Jeans. Here's how it works: buy them at least two inches too big (it's no wonder there's not a women's equivalent); let them soak in really hot water, drip dry, towel dry, then *put them on while they're wet*; wear them until they're dry. As the jeans dry, they conform to your body's shape and size.

Church systems are like jeans. You can build a great system that works perfectly for your size and context, and it'll have a little give at first. But as your congregation continues to grow in number and volume of care needed, there's only so much stretch. Eventually, the congregation will outgrow the system, or the congregation will grow *down* to the size of the organizational system.

That's how I see the Congregational Care Ministry, which was born out of the large United Methodist Church. The care and concern ministry leadership built a system that was sustainable for tens of thousands of people. The way they organized their various groups that fell under the care ministry, and the way they documented it all was a couple "sizes" too large for our context, and if Bill and I would have attempted to replicate that same system in our appointments, it would not have worked. That is why it was so vital for us to inventory the actual needs of our congregation and start with the basics. We created a plan to gradually build our care system, and I invite you to do the same.

Starting Fresh

Two years after we established the Congregational Care Ministry in our first church, my husband, Bill, and I were appointed to co-pastor another church in our conference. The church was quite a bit larger with a higher average worshipping age (and therefore more care needs), but the care model still relied on care provided solely by the pastors. We knew it was an unsustainable model, and we needed to move swiftly to establish a Congregational Care Ministry within the church in order for the church to stabilize and ultimately grow. We followed Rev. Karen Lampe's evaluation model: establishing phases within the first five years.

Year One

During the first year, *recruit and train your team as you evaluate* what care needs are most important for your congregation. Where are you sensing urgency, anxiety, or frustration from the congregation? What types of prayer requests are you receiving the most? Evaluate your systems for prayer request intake and begin building the need for a Congregational Care Ministry (see next chapter for tips on building the need).

Evaluate your congregation's needs and the care/support classes or groups that already exist in your congregation. What works? What doesn't?

What needs to be pruned? What is missing? You should ask these questions each year as you continue to evaluate.

The first month in our new appointment, we listened and learned. We met with congregants, made hospital and nursing home visits, and tried our best to connect with the community. We learned that the town had a wonderful health care system and that many people chose to move to the town after retirement because of the care and nursing facilities. Many long-time members had grown into the life stage that limited their mobility and relegated them to their homes. We also learned that prayer requests were by word of mouth, spoken out loud during prayer time on Sunday mornings, or calls to the pastors' personal cell phones.

During our listening phase, we observed a sense of anxiety that prayer requests would slip through the cracks—and they did. We observed a sense of urgency as congregants would leave voicemails for non-emergency prayer requests in the evenings and on weekends. We also perceived a deep need for face-to-face interaction for those who were bound to their homes or a nursing facility. The need for care was high, and there was no system in place to guarantee quality care for our people. We did the math: if Bill and I worked around the clock with no breaks or days off, we still would have had only twelve minutes to devote to those who had care needs each week.

We determined that the most critical needs at the time related to prayer request intake and visiting the elderly population bound to their homes or nursing facilities, and we got to work. We enlisted someone at each worship service to write down the prayer requests spoken out loud with the names of the requesters (remember, we were new and didn't know most of the people yet). We had no way of knowing how to follow up until we enlisted our volunteer who did know the congregation. What a help! In the meantime, we developed prayer request cards and added them into the pew backs. Every Sunday, when we moved into prayer time, we reminded the congregation to write their requests down on those cards and place them into the offering plate if they wanted a follow-up call (even if they lifted up their request out loud in the service). We were honest with them that we needed help remembering names and keeping all the care needs organized. We also began publicly building the need for a Congregational Care Ministry early on (guidelines for this are in the following chapter), and we identified laypeople in our congregation who exhibited gifts of compassion and care. We began recruiting our first class of CCMs at the church, and by month four into our appointment, they were commissioned and began offering care on behalf of the church.

I want to stress this major point: empower great people. It will help your ministry thrive. I've seen pastors try to do it all or not play ball with their colleagues. Share the joy, empower people to use their gifts, and help them pass the baton to one another. I liken a good ministry team to a sports team: it has the right people in the proper positions. They call upon one another and help one another become great players. Having a team is so much easier than going it alone. Plus, you will be sustained and supported in your ministry.

Years Two and Three

In the second and third years of the plan, look at which ministries are working well, what needs to be pruned, and what needs to be created. Establish any care classes or groups that would be helpful care offerings for the community. Be sure to look outside the walls of the church as well. What resources does your community offer, and who might become partners in your work? Create a database of medical and mental health entities, support groups, Alcoholics Anonymous (AA) and Narcotics Anonymous (NA) groups, drug rehabilitation centers, hospice care centers, and so forth, and reach out to each of them. Share these contacts with your CCMs, so that they can refer care recipients to other resources in the community.

After some time living into a new system of care, we began looking beyond our visiting team. As we built trust with the congregation, we noticed the prayer requests became deeper and more personal. People in the congregation approached us about how to become a CCM, and others began wanting to create groups. A young man began leading an AA group in our church, and two women launched a Financial Peace class. Another woman pitched her idea of a prayer team. It was clear we needed to move beyond our core group of CCMs and expand. We commissioned a second class of CCMs to respond to the prayer requests by praying with them over the phone, and we established the prayer team, led by the woman who pitched the idea. All prayer requests submitted were shared with the prayer team, which met weekly to spend an hour in prayer together for the church, community, and the specific prayer requests.

We also began making more connections with folks in the health care and social services community during this phase, which became incredibly vital when a flood left our town completely cut off in all directions for weeks. Our church became a major player in the town's rebuilding efforts because of the connections we had made in the community. The following year, almost exactly, we began social distancing due to the COVID-19 pandemic. Our congregation had grown accustomed to our CCMs providing care on behalf of the church, and it was heartwarming to see that kind of attitude infiltrate our community. The voice of the CCMs brought calm and assurance through these uncharted times. Folks who were not CCMs picked up the phone and called one another to check in and pray. They organized a good old-fashioned phone tree, scheduled Zoom calls, sent cards, and left care baskets on people's porches. Individuals made fabric masks for others, ran errands for the elderly population, chalked driveways, and planted flowers for one another. This is what happens when pastors get out of the way and let the church be the church!

Years Four and Five

Years four and five, dream big, hairy, audacious dreams! Does your community need a recovery ministry? Perhaps you can develop a mental health ministry as you partner with other community groups. The idea is to keep dreaming!

As you continue to evaluate, we encourage you to think beyond the current realities and forecast for the future. What are the trends that will continue to rise? What are possible future roadblocks in the community, the congregation, and the ministry? What are future needs that you need to consider now in order to be prepared to address them when they arise?

During the COVID-19 pandemic and social distancing, we began dreaming about digital care and connection for those feeling isolated, while also keeping in mind the very bleak realities of the impending economic crisis, rates of unemployment, communal grief, and increases in addictive and destructive behavior patterns. We began planning for ways to address those very specific needs in our community. The needs are great for the church to rise up and provide a healing space for those who suffer.

Classes and Groups

As you continue to explore ways to care for your congregation, you may have people approach you about starting a group experience. We are constantly assessing the current needs of the congregation. Group ministry can be very beneficial because common experiences provide empathetic responses and teach others appropriate responses to others' needs. Groups can provide times to teach curriculum to large numbers of people, and it can be a time-saving way to minister to people who are facing similar situations.

How you conduct group ministry is important. Many times congregants will want to start a support or care group. Begin with a three-to-five-week class to gauge interest of the group. There is a great advantage in having a start date and an end date to the group. Having an end date is not typical of a support group, which can become unhealthy as people are allowed to linger in their circumstances instead of graduating and moving on.

Make sure you have good facilitators who are skilled at leading such a group. Set standards for them, such as checking in with you at least once a month through email or a debriefing session.

Help your leaders develop a curriculum that begins and ends with prayer, includes handouts, and has a definite spiritual component. People can find great secular resources outside the church, but most of the time they are coming to church to receive something they could not receive elsewhere. For instance, many hospitals provide grief care, but by coming to a church, the person expects that there will be a spiritual component. Many counselors provide support groups for those going through a divorce, but a divorce recovery group at a church will include a very nonjudgmental faith approach. The question to ask is, How does this group offered at the church differ from one offered in the community?

Once you have decided to have a group, publicize it in your usual ways (bulletin, newsletter, email, Facebook, and other social media). Go through lists of recent funerals to identify potential members of a grief class, keep your ears open for recent or difficult divorce situations, notice if there is an increase in parenting challenges, or if your community has been particularly hard hit by a slow economy and job loss.

You want your groups to succeed. These classes and groups must address the needs of *your* community. If the class experience is good, you may want to make it into a regular support group. Be cautious about calling it a support group, however, as that implies a long-term commitment.

I encourage you again to continually assess your congregation and community. There may be some great ministries ready to be born as you try to address ever-changing needs. It is vital that you stay alert, nimble, adaptable, and grounded in your own spiritual life in order to be effective in ministry.

How to Establish a New Group Ministry

Create a standard process to determine the need and appropriateness of a new group ministry. Ask questions designed to help those who are proposing the new group. The answers to these questions form the plan for the support group. Lay leaders are champions at such efforts. It is always important, though, to offer a chance for regular debriefing with the leaders. Encourage and praise them in their efforts. Consider the following questions:

1. What is the purpose of the proposed ministry?

    –   What does God want to accomplish with the proposed ministry?

- Describe how this group is in accord with our church's purpose and policies.

2. Whom will the new ministry serve?
   - Who is the primary audience for this ministry?
   - Who will benefit or be served?

3. Which needs will the new ministry serve?
   - Consider spiritual, physical, emotional, and relational needs.
   - What kind of services will the new ministry provide to meet these needs?

4. How will we provide those services?
   - What will be the ministry strategy for providing those services?
   - What will be the operational plan?
   - What is the process for providing the services?

5. Describe the leadership structure that the new ministry will require.
   - What are the various roles and responsibilities needed to support this ministry?
   - Describe the proposed structure of this ministry.

6. What resources will the new ministry require?
   - Identify training, facilities, computer access, mailboxes, need for staff assistance, finances, announcements, etc.

7. What is the vision for growth and expansion?
   - What growth is expected?
   - What is the "dream" for this ministry two years from now?

8. How will the effectiveness of this ministry be evaluated?
   - Include measurement systems that will gauge whether the ministry is successful in accomplishing its purpose. For ex-

ample, this could include measuring increases in the number of people in the group, or group evaluation forms.

9. Does the ministry already exist in the church?

 – Is there similarity between this ministry and one that your church already offers?

 – Should this new ministry be coordinated with other ministries?

 – Should this new ministry replace an existing one?

Assessing Your Community

In this chapter, we provided a framework for evaluation in which you are able to develop a five-year plan for care in your context. Consider the following questions as you implement the fourth essential.

o What are your church's current primary needs?

o What are your community's current primary needs?

o What resources already exist in the community that would be good to share with your CCMs?

o How might your church offer a faith-based response to those communal needs?

o What needs do you anticipate in your church and community in the coming years?

o What care groups already exist? What needs to exist? What needs to be pruned?

o What's your big, hairy, audacious dream for care in your community? hat would it take for that to become a reality?

Chapter Five

Fifth Essential: Build the Congregational Need

Commit your work to the Lord, and your plans will succeed.

—Proverbs 16:3

Early in our new appointment, my husband, Bill, and I (Melissa) realized that buy-in from the congregation was crucial to the development of the Congregational Care Ministry. The long-standing tradition of an ordained pastor making every care visit and call became an obstacle in the early stages of development that required thoughtful, theological maneuvering from the pulpit, in our internal communications, and in interpersonal conversations. It required strategic choices on our part as pastors with our leadership teams. We also discovered that thick skin and an unwavering commitment to healthy ministry systems played integral roles in establishing the ministry. It required finesse, compassion, persistence, and vision, committing wholly to the good of the entire community and not to the few loudest complainers.

It's one thing to establish a care ministry, recruit and train volunteers, dispatch and document, and continue to evaluate your ministry. It's a whole other thing to convince your congregation that the Congregational Care Ministry is the right choice for the congregation to support as well as for those seeking care through this new ministry method.

For decades, care has been a primary responsibility of the pastor, and in many cases, congregants expect the pastor to do all visits and care calls. We know that's not a sustainable model, but it is the ministry leaders' responsibility to help our congregations come to the same conclusion. In this chapter, you will find examples of how to build the congregational need through various channels in order to maximize the impact your Congregational Care Ministry can have in the community. All examples are real-life ones: we used these very words in our context to help build the congregational need in the face of opposition. We will also provide suggested time lines for a plan of action that includes a communications strategy to build the need strategically.

Conversations

One of the most strategic ways to gain buy-in is to have open and honest conversations with individuals about the need. In our case, we knew the workload was too much for us, and instead of pretending we could do it all and acting like we could handle it, we made it very clear that we were no heroes. When pastors allow themselves to be vulnerable, admitting to our own shortcomings and mistakes without beating ourselves up about it, we build trust with our congregation. They begin to see the humanity in a pastor rather than viewing them as the "hired help." Bill and I had conversations with individuals, but we also had strategic meetings with our leadership teams to remain open and transparent about where we were headed in our development of the Congregational Care Ministry. Consider having conversations with the following:

o **Staff/Pastor Parish Relations Committee (SPRC)**—This team oversees the work of the pastors and staff. Our conversation with the SPRC included strategic plans for other ministry initiatives we had, hours spent on care each week in relation to other ministry responsibilities, hours needed for new initiatives, honest evaluation of personal boundaries and sabbath, and presenting the Congregational Care Ministry model as a solution.

o **Church Council**—This team functions as the strategic body of the church, composed of representatives from all existing teams. Our conversation with the church council included SPRC's approval for the Congregational Care Ministry model and a deep dive into how the ministry will function, along with a reassurance that the pastors continue to provide care alongside CCMs.

o **Influencers**—All churches have those natural leaders whom others respect, even when they do not hold official leadership positions in the church. Often, since we were new to the church and community, these influencers reached out to us. Other times, we invited them to coffee or dinner. Our conversations included a short overview of our plans for the next phases of our ministry, including the vision for the Congregational Care Ministry. When you can gain the trust of the church influencers, they will publicly support and endorse the ministry.

o **Laity to Recruit**—Early on, we identified leaders who were already providing care to others in the congregation in some capacity. We invited those individuals to one-on-one coffee meetings, which included a transparent conversation about our need for help in providing adequate care on behalf of the congregation. We shared the vision for the Congregational Care Ministry and invited them to consider applying to be a CCM.

Church Communications

As you move toward commissioning your first class of CCMs, you must cast the vision for the ministry from the official internal communication channels of the church. For us, these included Sunday morning bulletins, a midweek eNote, and a monthly newsletter. We made sure to communicate clearly and succinctly, casting vision, defining the program, and sharing personal experiences to build the need. Bulletins included brief descriptions and images advertising our commissioning service. Midweek eNotes included a bit more description of the ministry, and the newsletter included the most text, providing a rationale for the ministry, along with details and plans.

From the Pulpit

Another way we built the need for our congregation was by hosting a "State of the Church Address," much like a town hall meeting for the church. We hosted one evening to share information and stories about ministry at the church over the previous year. We found that our congregation enjoyed hearing stories of how their ministry had impacted the community and each other, and it was a wonderful time to celebrate ministry that had already been done while looking to the future. We were able to cast vision for the Congregational Care Ministry, and once the ministry had been implemented, we made heroes out of our CCMs by telling stories of care and transformation.

Additionally, every single week, pastors have a somewhat captive audience for a block of time. We used that time to build the need and make heroes out of those who answer God's call to use their gifts. A key sermon series that drove the need home for a congregation was one called "Healing Wounds." We preached about all sorts of ways to make amends and care for our own hurt while reaching out to others. The last sermon was titled "Scar Stories," in which we explained how those who have gone through hurt can allow God to heal those wounds into scars. God then uses those scars to help heal others; we become wounded healers. That set us up to be able to discuss the Congregational Care Ministry model, which led into our commissioning service.

Commissioning Your CCMs

One of the best ways to help your congregation live into this new model of care ministry is to continuously champion your CCMs—in conversation, through storytelling, and from the pulpit. Once your CCMs have been trained, I encourage you to commission them publicly during a worship service in order to affirm their ministry. It is a sort of credentialing or endorsement in the eyes of the average layperson, and when the pastor lays hands on and prays a commissioning prayer over the CCMs, it becomes a very serious and solemn way to reinforce care ministers *as ministers.*

Choose a strategic time to commission. Consider when your congregation tends to reengage and attendance is higher. For us, we commissioned in the fall after school had started and before the holidays kicked into high gear. Other strategic times might include the beginning of the new year, right after Easter before the end of school year activities, at the end of a strategic sermon series about care, or right before a pastoral change. Pastors: give a gift to the pastor following you, and set them up for success!

Regardless of when you commission, ask every CCM to attend every worship service for commissioning so that they are visible to all. For those who cannot make that work, ask them to submit a photo to be displayed on a slideshow while the others stand onstage during commissioning.

Time Lines for Building the Need

The time line for establishing the Congregational Care Ministry in a local church depends largely on the pastor's current appointment. As you consider how you will strategically build the need in your context, consider the following time lines.

If beginning a new appointment . . .	
ASAP	Conversations about CCM with the SPRC at introductory meeting and following meetings. Get district superintendent/regional support prior to the introductory meeting, if possible. Request a list of names of possible CCMs from your SPRC or transition team.
July 1	New appointment start date
Month of July	Meet leaders; home gatherings to meet congregation in small groups

Month of August	Home gatherings; connect with possible CCMs, invite them to apply; begin building the need from the pulpit and at home gatherings
Month of September	CCM training
First Sunday of October	Commissioning
October—December	Weekly small group meetings with CCMs for support and continued education
November—December	Incorporate at least one "hero-making" CCM story into a sermon.
If mid-appointment . . .	
Current Quarter	Individual and team conversations. Build the need into at least one sermon. Connect with possible CCMs.
Next Quarter	Complete CCM recruitment. Train. Build the need into at least one sermon, providing more details about the upcoming Congregational Care Ministry.
Following Quarter	Commission CCMs. Utilize all internal church communications to continue communicating the new shift.
Last Quarter	Incorporate at least one "hero-making" CCM story into a sermon.

Assessing Your Community

In this chapter, we provided tangible examples for how to build the need for your Congregational Care Ministry into conversations, strategic team meetings, church communications, and from the pulpit. Now, it is your turn to develop your time line and strategy for implementing the fifth essential!

o   What will be your consistent messaging?

o   Who do you need to have conversations with?

o   Through which channels will you communicate the shift to the Congregational Care Ministry model?

o   How will you incorporate building the need into sermons?

o   What is your time line?

Part Two

Equipping Your Congregational Care Ministers

Essential Material for CCM Training

How to Use This Section

Congregational Care Minister training is a critical part of the Congregational Care Ministry. You cannot develop this ministry or offer your congregation appropriate care without a well-trained team of Care Ministers, no matter your church's size. Even a team of one or two people must receive the training.

This section of the book (Part Two: Equipping Your Congregational Care Ministers) provides the essential information you'll need for training CCMs. Each chapter covers a basic, foundational topic, and offers a variety of tools, methods, and techniques for CCMs to use. These chapters (6–12), along with *The Congregational Care Ministry: Care Minister's Manual*, provide the necessary material to create a training process. Here's what you need to know:

o   The CCM training must be designed and conducted in a way that makes sense for *your particular church*.

o   The pastor or other leader in charge of this Ministry should create a training process, using the chapters in this section as the foundation.

o   We strongly suggest you develop your training topics in the order of these chapters, from Theology to Documentation. It is especially important to begin your training with Theology.

o   Read through each chapter in this section and the corresponding chapter in the *Care Minister's Manual*. Decide what material will be most important for your CCMs (perhaps all of it!).

o   Draw from all the tools, methods, explanations, sample documents and instructions offered, in order to design effective training for your setting.

o   Carefully review the chapters in Part Three of this book, and Segments 7–10 in the *Care Minister's Manual*. These chapters address specific issues which may also be important for you to include in your training.

Chapter Six

Theological Foundations

*Gracious loving God, we come to you so grateful for the grace that you
freely give to us. You know everything about us and love us still! Help us to
embody your grace and love that surely we might provide a space of grace
for all who might need it. All this that your kingdom might come,
in Christ's name. Amen.*

The foundation for an effective care ministry is a consistent theology
that reflects not only a depth of understanding of the denominational
standards but also is ethical and thoughtful for the particular needs of the
people in the community. Best practices must consider not only scripture,
but reason, tradition, and experiences that model healthy boundaries.

Congregational Care Ministers represent the heart and hands of the
church. They are both pastoral as well as prophetic. They represent Micah
6:8 to do justice, love kindness, and walk humbly with God.

In practice, CCMs play important theological roles at different times, as

o   prophets offering guidance and leadership,

o   priests offering grace and mercy, and

o   physicians offering spiritual, mental, and physical care.

CCMs meet the people where they are offering Christlike healing to
all people.

Redemption

An understanding of redemption is key to Christian caregiving. The simple definition of redemption is "to restore." Restore to what? Restore to being the whole person God intends, a person who communes with God and whose character is marked by the fruits of the Spirit (Galatians 5:22-23). Good congregational care offers redemption as you partner with God to care for the weary, heavy-laden souls who are trying to hang on and cope.

Through acts of care, people can find restoration in the middle of death and grief or in simple acts of kindness. Redemption becomes the cornerstone for everything done through congregational care. A simple rule of thumb for pastors and CCMs is "grace + rules = redemption."

Understanding Christlike Healing

Throughout the biblical text, we read stories explaining the human condition where there is physical, spiritual, mental, and institutional pain. These stories teach us how God works in the world. Much of what is recorded in the scriptures reveals how God's redemptive, healing grace works to bring about restoration of individuals and relationships as well as institutional justice.

The stories, psalms, and prophetic voices of the Hebrew Scriptures were formational for the healing work of Jesus. He used scripture to help people understand that his ministry reflected the heart of God, which "heals the brokenhearted, and binds up their wounds" (Psalm 147:3 NRSV).

In Isaiah, the reader is given a glimpse of the character of the long-awaited savior with names such as a "great light" (Psalm 9:2 NRSV), "Wonderful Counselor" and "Prince of Peace" (Isaiah 9:6 NRSV), who "bring[s] good news to the oppressed . . . providing "a garland instead of ashes, the oil of gladness instead of mourning" (Psalm 61:1, 3 NRSV). This fearless leader is able to walk into the challenges of the time and is well acquainted with grief and sorrow (Isaiah 9; 43; and 53). As caregivers, we are called to this Christlike model.

In the Gospels, Jesus inspires us to a high standard of care that exemplifies his new covenant of grace for all. His "light" in the book of John is drawn to the downtrodden, the depressed, those kicked to the curb, and those physically ill. This prophetic ministry also included the larger community where he saw social injustices of all sorts, poverty, and unethical situations that moved him to action.

Then in Matthew 25 and John 21 we hear Jesus calling his followers to care for the least and the lost lambs. We hear his challenge to become caregivers in John 14:12 (NRSV) when he says, "The one who believes in me will also do the works that I do."

Anyone embarking on this journey of becoming a Christlike healer must constantly be in prayer that they might understand and follow the "way" of Christ.

Examining closely in the scriptures what this "way" looks like will inform our own capacity to facilitate healing and restoration.

There are five foundational items to consider.

1. Jesus was constantly in prayer.

2. Jesus literally got down in the dirt with people.

3. Jesus was willing to go the extra mile.

4. Jesus was wildly inclusive.

5. Jesus had a team of people.

Let us consider thoughtfully these five foundational precepts of the Christlike way.

Prayer

The life of Jesus was steeped in prayer as he was constantly leading people to have their sacred moments of connection with God as he went about listening, healing, creating, and bringing justice. He showed us that prayer lifts us up and out of the chaos of the moment to a different reality. That reality is where we connect with God and where redemption can happen. Prayer creates a holy and sacred space.

On rare occasions cited in scripture we see Jesus *receiving and experiencing* prayerful moments with others such as at his baptism (John 1:32-33) when John the Baptist baptizes Jesus and the Spirit comes to Jesus in the form of a dove. Another sacred moment was when the woman came to anoint Jesus with perfume. Different versions of this event are recorded in all four Gospels. A common denominator is that he declares to those who rebuke her that she is anointing his body for burial. Another holy narrative is the story of the transfiguration (Matthew 17) where Jesus shared time with three disciples while God spoke from a cloud as Jesus became dazzling white light.

All of these examples call us to seek a greater connection with God that will prepare us to be agents of God's healing love.

Before we walk into any healing situation, we must have taken our own time with God so that the spirit might more fully work through us.

As we go through this text, we will explore ways to build our prayer life as well as ways to use it through our ministry.

Down in the Dirt

In John 8:1-11, Jesus literally got down in the dirt when the woman who was accused of adultery was brought to him. Notice that only the woman was brought to Jesus and not the man. Notice that the accusers were ready to stone the woman as they were following the law in Leviticus 20:10.

The actions and posture of Jesus are important for us to consider as we think about our own ministry. In this complex story of sexual impropriety, Jesus got down in the dirt twice as he offers grace and compassion that point to a new covenant for the individuals involved as well as for the community. He was modeling for them a *nonjudgmental way of redemption.* He assured the woman that she was worthy of a second chance.

As we do ministry, are we ready to get down in the dirt, run into the fire, or step onto the turbulent waters? Jesus encourages us to believe that we can do all of this and more.

The Extra Mile

Sometimes in ministry we are asked to do more than we initially had thought we could do. Jesus understood that call where we find God leading him into places that were not the usual. In the story of the Samaritan woman in John 4:4 (NRSV), the scripture tells us he "had to go through Samaria" when in actuality the more usual way for Jews to travel from Judea to Galilee was to go through the Jordan River valley. This was the safer and quickest way. Yet Jesus felt the Spirit guiding him to go through Samaria to meet this woman who was struggling.

This woman had been married five times and felt so shamed that she would wait until all of the other women had come and gone from the community well. Yet Jesus asks her for a drink of water to remind her that this is a new way he is providing in breaking down old boundaries as he models a Jewish teacher asking a Samaritan woman for provision.

The scriptures tell us details about the conversation they had where he tells us details about her life while at the same time speaks with hope about the "living" water that he provides. I would imagine their conversation was much longer than what the scripture text provides. For to fully drink of this water that Jesus was offering, I would imagine that he listened to her tale of woe and how her life had not turned out as she had hoped. And then at some point he reveals to her that he is the messiah and that he had come clear to Samaria to offer her a new life. The woman went back to her village and, because of her testimony, there were many who believed.

There will be times in care ministry when you will be called to go the extra mile. *Your listening presence will offer healing beyond your comprehension.* Be assured that when you allow God to lead, there will be great blessings.

Wildly Inclusive

There are times when it would be so much easier to keep our conversation only with those whom we know are in agreement with us. Yet, the way of Jesus is wildly inclusive. Being a Jew, he understood that socially there were strict boundaries with societal norms. Jews did not mix with Samaritans. Women did not own property, hold office, teach, or even sit with the men. The ruling Romans did not mix with the general public. The class system was alive and well.

Jesus speaks and lives a new covenant to break down barriers so true healing can come to individuals as well as communities. Consider a few of these stories:

o   Jesus having supper with the despised tax collector, Zacchaeus (Luke 19:1-10),

o   Jesus healing those "unworthy" on the Sabbath (Luke 13:10-17; John 5:1-18),

o   Jesus healing the slave of a political foe (Luke 7:1-10), and

o   Jesus befriending Nicodemus, the Pharisee (John 3:1-21).

In caring ministries, there is an opportunity to *create a new collective consciousness* where the community provides a seat at the table for everyone. This may mean that you start new ministries for recovery from addiction, grief, mental health issues, elder care, LGBTQIA+ issues, divorce care, financial difficulties, and food insecurity. These are not easy ministries. But we do not ask for the easy way but rather what will usher in the kingdom of God.

The Team

From the very beginning of his ministry, Jesus sought to build a team of people who were up to the challenge. That being the case, he brought together a diverse group including fishermen, a tax collector, a zealot, and a thief. Alongside that there were three Marys who gave him immense support throughout his ministry. After his ascension, he continued to call people, including the Apostle Paul who had earlier killed the followers of Christ.

The idea here is to find people whose life stories help them relate to people who might be challenged in a number of different situations. CCMs are usually survivors themselves who were lifted up by the faith community. They have had their own moments of rising up out of the ashes. Their life stories ready them to do the healing ministry, leading others through their dark times to the light of Christ.

The development of our theology is essential to the foundation of our healing ministry. Our theology is born out of our understanding of scripture, reason, tradition, and our life experiences. As we consider the different challenges of our current times, the Christlike way will help us to create a space of love and grace where all people can flourish and grow.

Assessing Theology of Care

Preach the faith till you have it, and then,
because you have it, you will preach faith.

—Peter Bohler, speaking to John Wesley
(The Rev. Mr. John Wesley's Journal, vol. 1,
February 1, 1738, to September 16, 1738)

On what principles is your faith grounded? Do you use any or all of the following to answer your theological questions?

Scripture

How do you view and use scripture in your life and ministry?

What is the role of scripture in salvation?

Tradition

Do you see yourself standing on the shoulders of those who have gone before?

What do you understand about two thousand years of Christian tradition?

Who are the saints in your life?

Reason

In what ways do you love God with all your mind?

Do you tend to check your brain at the door of the church, turning off your powers of reason and critical thinking?

Experience

How has the Holy Spirit worked in your life?

What are some examples of times when you felt aware of the presence of the Holy Spirit? In what ways do you cultivate that awareness on a daily basis?

Practice using scripture, tradition, reason, and experience to address a current-day care need such as suicide or mental health situations. Write out your thoughts. Call this practice to mind daily, using it to consider different situations and needs. Begin to make this evaluative process a regular habit.

Three Simple Rules

John Wesley, founder of Methodism, taught three general guidelines to apply faith to everyday circumstances, including how we care for others. We encourage you to be mindful of the three simple rules in your ministry.

1. Do no harm.
2. Do good.
3. Stay in love with God.

Assessing Your Community

As you finish this chapter, take time to consider in groups these questions in the context of being a Christlike healer in your community:

o   How is the Christlike way lived out in your context?

o   How would you describe the collective consciousness regarding care of your faith community?

Chapter Seven

In All Things, Pray First!

Don't be anxious about anything; rather, bring up all of your requests to God
in your prayers and petitions, along with giving thanks. Then the peace
of God that exceeds all understanding will keep your hearts
and minds safe in Christ Jesus.

—Philippians 4:6-7

Prayer is the starting place for every ministry. Creating a vital congregational care ministry starts with prayer. That being said, sometimes we take the power of prayer for granted.

Every church and pastor have some basic ideas about the importance of prayer. Prayer is the means by which people expect the pastor to connect with God, yet so many times pastors are reticent to say, "I'd like to pray for you now. Would that be OK?" As leaders we should model and teach prayer as our key tool for care ministry.

Please allow me the opportunity to pray for you as we begin the chapter on prayer together:

O healing God, we give you thanks for the opportunity to serve your people. We
give you thanks for appointing us to this holy task. Yet we do not know and are
unsure of how to prioritize needs and create the systems that will best meet those
needs. So Lord, I pray for everyone who is starting this journey. Give them cour-
age and strength to know that you will guide them. Please provide them with

vision, understanding, and resources. Help them not be afraid to ask for help from you and others. In all of this, we give you the praise as we point your people to your healing grace and love. In Christ's name. Amen.

Transformation and Restoration

Prayer lifts us up and out of the chaos of the moment to a different reality. That reality is where we connect with God and where restoration can happen.

Prayer creates a holy and sacred space.

Prayer Is a Powerful Tool

o   in person

   –   public space

   –   private space

o   on the phone

o   in an email

o   in a handwritten note

When They Don't Have the Words

o   intercede for them with prayer (Romans 8:26-27)

o   model and teach them how to pray

Prayer, at its simplest, is talking to God. There is nothing magic in prayer—no specific formulas you have to follow or words you have to say. There are some things that make prayer easier, but the whole goal is to open ourselves up to God and share whatever is on our hearts with God. Prayer can be silent or out loud; it can be in a group, or solo. We pray out of gratitude for good things, or out of mourning for lost things—or even screaming prayers of anguish for troubling things.

Sometimes we pray to change God's mind—we ask God for miracles, and sometimes they do happen. Other times, we pray . . . and we hear silence. But we find that even when God doesn't answer how we want, that *God's presence begins to strengthen us for what is coming.* I've prayed for hundreds, maybe thousands of people when they were sick, or in hospitals—I can think of a few times when the person miraculously got better, and some who significantly outperformed the diagnosis . . . but most of the time, my prayer is for God to walk alongside the individual and family to provide strength, comfort, and assurance. Even Jesus didn't always get his first request, yet he was always seeking God's highest purposes. Shortly before he would be betrayed, tried, and eventually crucified,

> [Jesus] went, as was his custom, to the Mount of Olives; and the disciples followed him. When he reached the place, he said to them, "Pray that you may not come into the time of trial." Then he withdrew from them about a stone's throw, knelt down, and prayed, *"Father, if you are willing, remove this cup from me; yet, not my will but yours be done."* Then an angel from heaven appeared to him and gave him strength. In his anguish he prayed more earnestly, and his sweat became like great drops of blood falling down on the ground. (Luke 22:39-44 NRSV, emphasis added)

We pray for the times when it will get better, and also for God to be present in the times when it won't; for God's presence with the person, and the person's family, and the doctors, and so on.

> *Prayer invites God's presence to suffuse our spirits; God's will to prevail in our lives. Prayer might not bring water to parched fields, nor mend a broken bridge, nor rebuild a ruined city. But prayer can water an arid soul, mend a broken heart, rebuild a weakened will.*
>
> —Rabbi Ferdinand Isserman

Our prayers connect us and others to God. Sometimes miracles come—and always God hears our prayers.

Learning to Pray Aloud

Learning to pray aloud, and to be comfortable doing so, requires practice and some discipline, and sometimes just courage to do it as the Spirit leads you. All CCMs and key care leaders should be encouraged to pray out loud with others when appropriate. Many people are reluctant to pray out loud in a group or even with one other person. It is estimated that 75 percent of the population suffers from at least some glossophobia—the fear of public speaking. As leaders we encourage one another to practice praying publicly so that the ministry of the laity can be more fully unleashed.

The following tools contain detailed information for training CCMs, congregants, volunteers, and staff about praying out loud and through other means such as through an email, on the phone, or through other written correspondence.

Key activities to help one learn how to pray aloud include:

o   understanding different forms of prayer,

o   writing extemporaneous prayers, and

o   finding inspiration and language for written prayers.

Understanding Different Forms of Prayer

For most people, having an understanding of the elements of prayer is helpful. As you develop your own style of prayer, you will find yourself not covering all of the different parts of the different prayer styles every single time you pray. Just being genuine and connecting people to God is the primary goal. Three different styles of prayer include ACTS, Collects, and Praying Scripture.

ACTS

ACTS is a multi-subject prayer model that covers many various aspects of prayer. It is based on the acronym for Adoration, Confession, Thanksgiving, and Supplication, and it provides a helpful and easy-to-remember framework for praying. You may use your own words, moving through the ACTS categories. Here are some scripture references that illustrate the scriptural and theological roots of this prayer model:

Adoration

*"Let my whole being bless the Lord! / Lord my God, how fantastic you are!
You are clothed in glory and grandeur!"*

—Psalm 104:1

Confession

*"For this reason, confess your sins to each other and pray for each other so that
you may be healed. The prayer of the righteous person is powerful in what it
can achieve."*

—James 5:16

Thanksgiving

*"Whatever you do, whether in speech or action, do it all in the name of the
Lord Jesus and give thanks to God the Father through him."*

—Colossians 3:17

Supplication

*"We pray our prayers for help to you, not because of any righteous acts of ours
but because of your great compassion."*

—Daniel 9:18

The Collect

A collect (pronounced *câh-lect*) is a one-subject prayer that comes from Christian traditions in which worship is more formally structured, such as the Catholic, Anglican, Episcopal, and Lutheran traditions. It is a short general prayer of a particular structure. The Book of Common

Prayer has many collects in the text. Many times, the words and phrases flow together into one poetic thought.

The collect is especially useful to the pastor or caregiver to pray before entering a hospital room or before meeting with a congregant. For example, in The Book of Common Prayer under the section addressing visitation of the sick, one collect reads: "O God, the strength of the weak and the comfort of sufferers: Mercifully accept our prayers, and grant to thy servant the help of thy power, that his sickness may be turned into health, and our sorrow into joy; through Jesus Christ our Lord. Amen." Notice the simplicity and how it works:

The collect has six parts:

1. *Invocation:* Call upon God by name. It can be simple, as in "Dear God," or more complex, such as "Breath of Life."

2. *Attribute of God:* Name an attribute of God that fits the petition. In the visitation prayer for the sick, the attribute is "the strength of the weak and the comfort of sufferers."

3. *Petition:* What one thing only are you asking God to do? In the visitation prayer it is "mercifully accept our prayer and grant thy servant help."

4. *Purpose:* The "so that" or anticipated result. In our prayer it is that the "sickness may be turned into health, and sorrow into joy."

5. *Closing:* This is a praise word or the basis for asking, as in "through Jesus Christ, our Lord."

6. *Affirmation:* "Amen." "So be it." "Let it be." Those who are listening can join in saying this.

Example: "Dear Creator God, who healed people who were sick in body and spirit, heal Mary from shingles and reduce her pain, so that she can serve you better and care for her family. With grateful hearts we pray, in Jesus's name. Amen."

This type of prayer is such a helpful element of daily care calls because it helps you meet each person with an understanding of the importance of the minutes you have with them. It allows you to express their deepest concerns. One addition that is always helpful in this model is to add an expression of gratitude or thankfulness to God.

Praying Scripture

One of the beautiful practices a pastor or care volunteer can learn and use is the blending of scripture with prayer. If you have ever read any of the great essays of theologians, you can see how the words of scripture seem to flow easily out of them into their writings or prayers. When you know your scriptures, that is exactly what begins to happen as we pray with people. A scripture text will come to your mind and you find the words flowing out. People recognize these scriptures and many times these prayers can be such a help.

o   Read a scripture aloud slowly.

o   Pause in silence. Contemplate the passage. What is God saying? (If nothing, that's OK. Not all verses speak all the time.) How would you paraphrase this passage?

o   Read the passage aloud again. Pause in silence.

o   Write down the portion that stops you because it touches your heart.

o   Write your response to the portion of the reading that touched you. You may turn it into a simple prayer.

o   Read Psalm 46 to a congregant, specifically the words of "Be still, and know that I am God!" (v. 10 NRSV); you can incorporate that scripture into the prayer with something like, "Lord God, help us quiet ourselves that we might truly hear what you are speaking into our lives, so that no matter what happens we can be assured that you are with us."

o   At a bedside reading of the Twenty-Third Psalm (v. 4 NRSV), you can appropriately use the words "Even though I walk through the darkest valley, I fear no evil; for you are with me."

Other scriptures that you can easily commend to prayer are Isaiah 43:1 (NRSV), "Don't fear"; Jeremiah 29:11 (NRSV), "I know the plans I have in mind for you"; 1 Peter 5:7 (NRSV), "Throw all your anxiety onto him, because he cares about you." When you have a few of these scriptures in your repertoire and dwell on them in your own prayer time, you can easily weave the words of scripture into your prayers. This adds another dimension to the gift of prayer that you share with people.

Writing Extemporaneous Prayers

Writing prayers down on paper is one of the best ways to begin to learn how to pray out loud. Just because your prayer is not extemporaneous does not mean that it is not a heartfelt prayer. Writing out prayers helps clarify and organize your thoughts. It is also a spiritual discipline that helps you grow in prayer.

It is also helpful to know that the prayers that you write are replicable. If you are called upon to pray without any preparation, you can use one of the prayers that you have written or have said many times over and over. A good example of this is praying at the hospital bedside. If you visit people in the hospital, your prayer for one person or another will most likely be similar. You do not have to come up with an original prayer for each new person.

While intercessory prayer for someone else is essential there are other types of written prayers that don't ask God for anything, but simply express to God what is going on in your heart. God knows you in entirety and your thoughts and feelings are important to God. Many times such prayers can be written and expressed in a prayer journal. It can be a very cathartic action to write or type your prayers. This can become a way of releasing your fears and anxiety. Encouraging others to write their prayers can be a very helpful tool for their healing.

Sometimes writing prayers may include a scripture such as a psalm or words of scripture that inspire. Psalm 139:1-4 is one such example: "Lord, you have examined me. You know me. You know when I sit down and when I stand up. Even from far away, you comprehend my plans. You study my traveling and resting. You are thoroughly familiar with all my ways. There isn't a word on my tongue, Lord, that you don't already know completely."

Two other examples of prayers from the Psalms that express deep emotion are Psalm 8 (a psalm of praise) and Psalm 13 (a psalm of lament).

o   Notice the many emotions that these psalms express.

o   Compare and contrast the psalms using different translations or paraphrases.

o   See how different translations of the Bible reveal different nuances of emotion.

Notice how Psalm 8 praises the goodness and grandeur of God, and then how Psalm 13 cries out to God in anger and frustration in the midst of pain and suffering, but at the end the psalmist expresses God's faithfulness through hard times. Psalms of lament typically end their cries of sadness by changing perspective and recalling the goodness of God. Using a blank sheet of paper, spend the next two minutes writing a prayer like a letter to God. Write whatever emotions you are feeling or whatever you would express to God using everyday language.

Finding Inspiration for Prayers

It is not "cheating" to write down a prayer or to use a composed prayer from a source other than your own head and heart. If a written prayer expresses what you want to say, then it becomes your own also. A beautifully written prayer can be a good way to begin a circle of group prayer, say grace before meals, give comfort during an illness or following a great loss. Ready-made prayers like the Lord's Prayer or the Twenty-Third Psalm can resonate deeply within a person's memory. On D-Day the soldiers waiting in the boats to go ashore joined together in the Lord's Prayer. Patients who are suffering from memory loss will be able to call up these prayers.

Begin to develop your own library of prayer books that inspire you with their words and tone. Many times such books will help give you words before you walk into particular situations.

Don't be afraid to search the internet for prayers, particularly for a special occasion. You may find a prayer you want to use "as is," or inspiration that can help you write your own prayer. Looking through the different sources can inspire you to find appropriate words that will distinguish people of other denominations and faiths.

Key Ways to Receive and Extend Prayer

Four distinct ways to receive and extend prayer include:

o   prayer requests received from worship and online requests,

o   note writing,

o   prayer vigils and holy spaces, and

o   self-care.

Prayer Requests in the Bulletin or Online

These are so important to the congregation, and the logistical nature of prayer request intake is addressed in the documentation chapters. Whether a person has a new baby, faces a life-threatening disease, or sends a loved one off to war, people want to enlist their community of faith to pray with them.

Confidentiality is always a high priority as the church seeks to be highly sensitive to the needs of the faith family and the community.

Note Writing

Note writing has become a lost courtesy in today's instant messaging world. A handwritten note shows the reader that you care enough about him or her to invest in writing a personal note. To get started, create a rough draft of what you want to say. Think about what you might say in a face-to-face conversation, and then write it down.

1. Pray first! Ask God to give you his thoughts and attitude about the person and situation. Ask God to use your words to bless the person to whom you are writing.

2. Include the date or day of the week in the upper right-hand corner of the note.

3. Start the note with "Dear _____," rather than "hello" or "hi."

4. If the note is based on a prayer request, thank the person for submitting the request.

5. Acknowledge the loss, health concern, addiction, or other problem mentioned in the prayer request.

6. Express your sympathy for the loss of a loved one, your concern about a health situation, or other issues.

7. Try to put yourself in the position of the one receiving the note. What would you want someone to say to you?

8. Be brief. Keep the note simple. Use short sentences and descriptive words.

9. As the Spirit leads, give a scripture reference or verse to encourage him or her.

10. Avoid trite phrases such as "it's all for the best," "give it time," "your mother is in a better place" (even if that is true). Also avoid attributing the loss or problem as God's will.

11. Your words reflect your theology.

12. Assure people they are not alone. Tell them they are in your thoughts and prayers. Offer specific help, such as whom to call for additional prayer or guidance.

13. Close your note with "in Christ's love," "Grace and peace," or simply, "Blessings."

Useful Phrases for Notes

Condolences

Sympathy on the loss of your dear_____.

We are/I am praying for you.

We are available to walk with you on this journey.

Condolence after a Long Illness

We believe that _____is whole and happy and with God.

We believe that _____was welcomed into heaven.

We believe _____heard, "Well done, good and faithful servant."

Please call if you are having a rough time. Holidays, birthdays, and other special occasions may be hard to get through.

Health

May you feel the loving touch of Jesus, the Healer.

Praying you will recover and resume normal activity.

Praying you will recover after rehab, either in- or outpatient (e.g., in the case of stroke, joint replacement, etc.).

Praying for a speedy and uneventful recovery.

Please give yourself time to heal.

Remember to be patient and kind to yourself.

We are looking forward to seeing you back in worship (choir, Sunday school, Bible study, etc.).

Prayer Vigils and Holy Spaces

These are wonderful ways to draw people together to pray. A church might consider having two major vigils each year, one on Thanksgiving and the other on Good Friday.

o   Start the vigil early in the morning and continue through the evening.

o   Set up a welcome table outside the appointed site for the vigil. Decorate with a either a cross, candles, or seasonal flowers, or all of these. Lay out prayer guides for adults and children. Have prayer walk maps and guides available. Ask CCMs and staff to volunteer to serve at this table throughout the vigil in two-hour shifts.

o   Encourage small groups, Sunday school classes, or families to pray together.

o   Incorporate a short noontime program and end the day with a meaningful closing service.

o   Plan a prayer walk either in the church or around the church property, or both, with prayer stations and a prayer walk guide.

o   Print out names of congregants individually or as families. This may take two or three or fifty sheets of paper, depending on the size of your congregation. Give one sheet of names to each person attending the vigil, with instructions to pray for those on the list. The sheet should be initialed and returned to the welcome table.

Create holy spaces that encourage prayer. To learn more about holy spaces, visit other churches in your area to see strategic places set aside for prayer. If possible, have a special space set aside from the main sanctuary that is available daily for prayer or Communion. Other possibilities include:

o   Consider building a prayer wall in a quiet outdoor space that is protected from the wind and direct public view. Provide a bench or chairs. Encourage people to tuck written prayers between the stones. Have a staff member collect those requests for the covenant prayer team.

o   Supply an indoor holy space with Bibles, writing materials, prayer guides, candles, and chairs.

o   Provide reading materials that provide guidance regarding life issues, such as grief, miscarriage, divorce, unemployment, and so on.

Self-Care through Prayer

Personal Prayer Lists

As you begin to take on the duties of care, you will quickly recognize that the care will not have an off button. Once you know a person or family is walking through a challenging time, you will feel connected to their situation. As this mental list begins to grow, write down your list of prayer concerns. This allows you to actually note what their concerns might be and hopefully will help you release your concerns to God. For instance:

o   If you know that a family is dealing with an impending death, you can begin to intentionally pray for that family's well-being.

o   If there is a particular member of the family who seems to be dealing with guilt of unresolved issues, your prayers can provide guidance and strength for you as the caregiver about how you might lean into the situation, or perhaps be on guard so that you are not pulled into the cycle of guilt.

o   Most important, pray for God's unconditional love and grace to be poured out over each situation. Prayer is a powerful tool in this way.

Remember that God is always acting and we do not have to overfunction. God is the Savior. Allow God to work in God's perfect timing.

Prayer Practice for Self-care

In all of these ways that we have talked about prayer, we have not emphasized enough how important it is for us to wait upon God for our own self-care. Do you find yourself bogged down with the decisions and burdens of ministry?

Taking personal devotion time to connect with God seems to be a common problem that weary caregivers skip over. Your prayer life is vitally important to your total welfare. You are hardwired for your response to be either fight-or-flight. This keeps you safe when danger appears. However, you don't want to stay in that mode; rather, you need to pray and release anxieties. Prayer and meditation allow you to make an intentional shift away from those emotions that can keep you wound up tight in an unhealthy place. Ask yourself:

o   When do you sit silently before God?

o   How much time do you spend in quiet prayer, clearing your mind and waiting for God to speak?

No doubt Jesus understood how important his prayer time was as he experienced the rigors of ministry. We remember the story of Jesus in a crowd of people when he feels the power being drawn from him as a woman touches his garment. In our daily ministries we will come into contact with a multitude of needs and issues to be addressed. Like Jesus, we will feel the energy being drained from us. Yet we can also feel the power being shared with us as Jesus moves past us and we reach out for the hem of his garment.

When we look at the example of Jesus, we find him regularly going to the garden, the mountaintop, the wilderness, and the lakeshore to reconnect with God through prayer. We may not have the luxury of going to the garden, but we might find a quiet place in our closet or at our kitchen table with a candle burning. We must build a disciplined life of prayer to be able to do this healing ministry.

About eight years ago, I found myself really depleted from the daily demands of ministry. One of our CCMs who is a professional counselor encouraged me to talk to someone who had taught meditation through-out the city. I have to confess I put it off for a while (too busy, right?), but the first time we met I knew that whatever she had I needed. There was a sense of peace and grace within her that was nearly palpable. We have been meeting every Wednesday since I first met her. This disciplined life of prayer has revived my ministry. The prayer practices that we share remind me so much of the language that we find in the Gospel of John. Below is one such practice. A few simple steps before you begin the prayer include:

o   Sit for a moment in silence. Take four deep breaths. Breathe slowly and deeply from your abdomen. Fill your lungs. Shallow breathing increases tension; deep breathing relaxes.

o   What is the name of God that brings you greatest comfort (God, Jesus Christ, Father, Creator, Holy One, and so on)?

o   What is your greatest need (peace, strength, hope, healing, guid-ance, comfort, love)?

o   Combine the answers into a breath prayer for yourself.

o   Take several deep breaths, focusing on your breathing.

o   With your eyes closed, combine the name (breathe in) with the request (breathe out).

Breath Prayer Practice

A four-step personal breath prayer practice is a prayer tool to help anyone who is in ministry or those going through a challenge. Many times humans begin to hold their stress, fear, anxiety or pain in their bod-ies. The Breath Prayer allows you to name those negative emotions and then release them through the breath practice in step three. Plan to spend about five minutes on each segment, and perhaps a bit more on the last one. Give yourself twenty to twenty-five minutes for this exercise. Build this prayer practice into your daily disciplines for twenty-one days and you will find yourselves developing a new habit. This practice can offer healing spiritually, physically and mentally!

1. I acknowledge my feelings,
Remembering we are all human.
Am I feeling angry, resentful, fearful, anxious, and so on?
What are the lower emotions that I usually have?
Just be aware, don't judge.
Do these emotions serve God, others, yourself?

2. In this moment, I am feeling _____.
But this is not who I am.
I am not this anger, resentment, fear, and so forth.
I am a child of God.
My soul is connected to God.
I can choose to be different.
I choose to distance myself from the lower emotions.

3. Focus on your breath.
Breathe in and hold.
Breathe out and hold.
Visualize your breath as the light of Christ coming into your body.
The light comes into your mind, your eyes, your mouth.
The light goes down into your throat, heart, stomach, and out
into your arms and legs.
The light of Christ expands in your center as you hold your breath
and then release it.
Hold the focus on the light.

4. Visualize yourself as light, then do the same with peace, love, joy,
grace, and compassion.
Take time to center yourself in each of these higher attributes.
Breathe in each attribute fully and slowly.
Visualize yourself walking into any situation carrying God's light,
love, peace, grace, joy, and compassion.
I am light, love, peace, joy, grace, compassion.
I fully surrender myself to God.
Breathe in and out.

The purpose of experiencing silence in prayer is to welcome God's presence, allowing the divine light to dwell in you more fully.

Other tips to help you develop your personal prayer practice:

o   Find places where you can remove yourself to be alone and undistracted. Turn off phones, music, and any other noise-making device. Resolve not to respond to a knock on the door, the chime of emails, or that overwhelming urge to clean your closets or attic.

o   Set a timer for twenty minutes.

o   Take time to become completely silent in your head and spirit. Concentrate on your own breath or the sound of wind moving past you. Do not think in words or pray, just enter into God's presence and sit quietly.

o   Silent prayer is a time to take the focus away from yourself, your needs, and your petitions—even for other people. You need to be quiet and experience sitting with the Holy Spirit, turning your mind to the light of Christ. Acknowledge negative emotions and visualize dropping them into a fire. Do not dwell on them or try to name them—just take the feeling and get rid of it.

o   Let your arms rise above your head as the light of Christ rises up in you. Then let your arms spread open as the light of Christ flows out of you. Repeat this step several times. Experience yourself embodying light.

o   At the end of twenty minutes, end your silence in praise and thanksgiving for God's presence in your life and in this time together.

My prayer for you, dear ones, is to take time with God. Give God space and time to truly speak into your life. Use your breath prayer during those times. As you sit quietly, become aware of that peace, joy, or love that you requested. Breathe it in. When we take this important time, we receive what we need to be sustained in caring ministry. We are able to hear God say, "All is well."

Peace I leave with you. My peace I give you.

—John 14:27a

Practice Time!

If you are reading this as part of a team or group, pray for one another. Break up into groups of five, and pray for one another. You can go in a circle and pray for the person to your right, or you can do it popcorn style, whatever works for your group. Pray for the weekend, for the person's gifts and that they may use the gifts God has given them, or pray for something going on in their life. But spend time in prayer. Debrief afterward.

BEST PRACTICES

Prayer of preparation: before every counseling session, pastors and CCMs are encouraged to pray. This prayer of preparation allows you to care for yourself spiritually, emotionally, and mentally, as you understand the rigors of such a session. This gift to yourself must not be neglected!

The Redemptive Force of Prayer

Redemption means the act of restoring. The importance of prayer for redemption in all situations is primary. Let me illustrate through a personal story: my own need of prayer.

Redemption Story: Karen's Story

Easter Sunday had finally arrived. That morning promised to be one of the best Easter Sundays ever for our church. The weather was exceptional, spring break was over, and the sports schedule was minimal. However, the week before had been brutal in other ways. Our department tended to the needs of eight families in the congregation who had experienced a death. For three of those funerals, I had been the lead pastor to attend to the services and the families. On Easter Sunday, I felt charged for the day, but I have to say I was running on near-empty.

I arrived at the church before our earliest service at 7:00 a.m., parked along the far edges of the parking lot, and began to walk toward the church. My robe, stole, two clean shirts, two pairs of shoes, and two bags of other needed items filled my arms. As I walked briskly—nearly breaking into a jog—I felt myself begin to stumble. As I continued at my quick pace, I completely lost my balance and went face-first toward the pavement. The left side of my face ate gravel and my glasses gave way. I thought, "This is not good."

Lying there, I hoped someone had seen the fall, yet in my embarrassment, I also hoped no one had seen me plummet. I picked myself up and quickly realized blood was coming from my mouth and nose, and I had scrapes up to my left eye.

I was taken by ambulance to the nearest hospital. The prayers that occurred in between the time the accident happened until I returned home around 1:00 p.m. revealed something about prayer and the restoration that happens through the redemptive process. Here briefly are a number of prayers that someone said for me or I said for someone else that Easter morning:

- The medical doctor who volunteers his care for our congregation during worship services prayed for me and I prayed for him.
- Our pastors came and prayed over me individually before I was taken to the hospital.
- On the way to the hospital I prayed for the young EMT in the ambulance who told me she and her partner could not find a welcoming church.
- I prayed with the custodian in the ER who said he was working three jobs and would not make it to church on Easter Sunday.
- My husband and I prayed with the young man who shared our large room in the ER. He shouted that he was scared and asked us to open the curtain separating us.

Whenever someone was praying for me or I was praying for someone else, we were in the act of restoring. We were transcending the chaos of the moment and connecting with God—where restoration can happen.

That crazy Easter morning that I will never forget was full of op-portunities for people to be touched by God's love—including me! After that morning, I received many calls, cards, social media mes-sages, and emails from people telling me they were praying for me. I truly believe those prayers accounted for why I healed so quickly.

Assessing Your Community

As a CCM, you are going to go into people's homes, hospital rooms, and funeral homes and sit at gravesites and walk with people through the deepest hells they have experienced. This is holy and important work. Prayer is your most important tool.

o   What is your daily prayer routine?

o   What does it mean for you to pray without ceasing?

o   What routine activities might give you daily prompts to pray?

o   Enlist a colleague or trusted congregant to discuss:

  –   Your content and prayer strategy.

  –   What is working?

  –   Why do you think it is working?

  –   What is not working?

  –   How can that be improved?

  –   Name steps for designing a strategy to follow on prayer requests.

o   Do you have a prayer team that regularly follows up prayer requests?

  –   If not, how could you develop one?

  –   How could your ministry benefit from an increased focus on prayer?

  –   When have you seen redemption happen though a personal illness or injury?

Chapter Eight

Boundaries

Carry each other's burdens and so you will fulfill the law of Christ.

—Galatians 6:2

Boundaries are the limits or borders we place on relationships, which allow us to balance closeness and freedom. Boundaries can exist to safeguard as well as to delineate what is acceptable and unacceptable behavior. When you are ministering to another person, not only do you need to respect his or her boundaries but you must also set boundaries for your relationship with him or her. Remember as a pastor or CCM, you are legally considered to be the person of authority, which means we must each consider every interaction.

Key Ideas to Consider and Discuss with Your Team

Be aware of your emotions.

Be cautious about sharing your personal information.

o   This will confuse your role—you will be seen as a friend, not a caregiver.

o The person might take on your worries.

o Don't share about yourself because you feel the need to talk.

o Only share information if it would be helpful for encouragement or as a teaching example.

o Seek care, counsel, and support for yourself.

o Be aware of your emotional responses/reactions.

o A person's strong emotions may trigger your emotions.

o It is normal to feel sadness, annoyance, fear, attraction, frustration, protectiveness, or sympathy.

o It is not helpful to express or act on these reactions.

o Give care and attention regardless of an emotional reaction. This takes practice!

o Be aware of your actions.

Touch

o Use sparingly.

o Can be a powerful tool.

o Can be healing and comforting or confusing, hurtful, and unwelcome.

o Use only when it serves a good purpose—the person's needs, not your own.

o Ask permission first.

o The person may react differently than you intend.

o Imagine your conversation is videotaped. How would you feel watching it, having your spouse watch it, or the other person's spouse watch it?

Tone of Voice and Words

o   The tone and volume of your voice reflect your emotions.

o   Ask them how they would like to be addressed, by first name or more formally?

o   Notice tones that convey frustration as well as those that are encouraging.

o   You can choose to care through the sound of your voice.

o   Calling them "sweetie" or "honey" may be offensive or blur the lines between professional and personal.

o   Ask someone to pay attention to your voice after you respond to different situations. You might not notice any change, but the listener likely will.

o   Focus on the person's needs, not personality.

o   A good teaching tool for a group discussion is to read *The Bridge*, a fable written by Edwin H. Friedman (published by The Guilford Press, 1990). It will reveal how vulnerable humans can be in their interactions with other people.

Basic Rules for Good Boundaries

Here are some basic boundary guidelines for anyone in support ministries:

o   Never allow yourself to be in an unsafe or compromising situation. Make sure windows have been installed in the doors of rooms used for meeting with congregants. Never care for someone alone in your church.

o   Understand that you are in a position of authority when you are caring for someone.

o Be cautious about where you meet to give care so that you can create a safe and professional setting. Seek guidance and support if you are to travel with a person for whom you are caring.

o Never go to a home visit alone if it may put you in a dangerous situation.

o Insist that all volunteers and staff take a course that teaches clear ethical boundaries set by your denomination. (States often have certification for people who provide childcare and adult day and nursing care.) Make certain this training includes conducting a legal background check on participants. Many denominations use a course called "Safe Gatherings."

o Teach and set standards for clothing for staff and volunteers. When people are in a vulnerable situation, do not let clothing detract from the sacred moments where you are entrusted to lead or listen.

o Be aware of any sexual feelings that you might have for a congregant, staff member, colleague, or volunteer. Acknowledge those feelings to yourself. But never acknowledge these feelings to the person who is the object of the feelings. Do not put yourself in a vulnerable position. Debrief with someone safe and keep your feelings in check.

o It is never appropriate to be in a romantic relationship with a person for whom you are caring.

o Never share a person's personal information.

o HIPAA protects the privacy of a person's health information. Churches are exempt from HIPAA, but, as caregivers, you must diligently guard the confidentiality of your congregation.

Practice

Work in threes to role-play setting safe boundaries. One person will be the caregiver, another person is seeking care, and the third person is the observer.

Possible Scenarios

- o a pregnant college-aged student
- o an angry wife who is living in an abusive relationship
- o a young person unemployed and depressed
- o a father or mother of three young children who was just diagnosed with cancer
- o a young person whose mother died tragically

Using the guidelines for boundaries, the evaluator will report on the setting, the emotions, the tones of voice, the use of touch, the effect on the caregiver, and the risk to the caregiver.

- o How did the caregiver set boundaries?
- o How did the person seeking care react to boundaries?
- o When were the boundaries pushed or breached? How did the caregiver react?
- o How did the caregiver manage the strong emotional atmosphere? If there is time, change roles and repeat this training.

Redemption Story: A Young Woman's Story

The young woman came into my office with a pained expression. She shyly shook my hand then sat down on the far side of the sofa. As we began our session, I went through my regular explanation about God's grace. She started to tear up but offered only silence when I asked if she had any questions before she began to tell her story. I offered a brief prayer and then asked her to share what was on her heart.

During an internship the previous summer, a trusted male supervisor began to take special interest in her. One night when they were alone, he assaulted her. Confused, ashamed, and not knowing what to do, she kept the incident to herself. But the scenario repeated itself with new drama time after time. When she found herself pregnant, she told her parents.

The story became more complex. She had not filed for any child support and had little interaction with the man after he learned she was pregnant. Apparently, he had urged her to get an abortion, but she refused. At the time she came to see me, the baby had been born, and she did not know how to move forward with her life.

Many women in such situations have a difficult time identifying abuse when it is happening. Often the behavior intensifies so gradually that it may not seem inappropriate until it has gone too far. Predators will take advantage of people of any age, and most predators do not realize their own sickness until they are called out on it in a big way.

In this particular instance, the young woman was so full of shame that it was clear we needed to pray about her own need for grace. The theological story of grace is made clear in Romans 5–8, which ends with the assurance that nothing can separate us from the love of God in Christ Jesus our Lord.

The young woman had several sessions with me as we talked about grace and justice. Also important to her journey was the need for a psychological counselor. She received psychological and spiritual counsel that I truly believe helped her.

This young woman is ever so much wiser, and is using her story to help others. She has even told her story on national television. Hopefully, many can learn from her story of the terrible offense her supervisor made and the amazing choices she made. This young woman has now graduated from law school and will forever be an advocate for women. This is the power of redemption!

Review and Discuss the Essentials

In every situation there may be larger issues that need to be considered. A CCM should always consult with their pastor to avoid any confusion or missteps about a situation. Many times, hard choices will need to be made and sometimes the best choice may not be perfect but will still be the best choice. Consider how rules + grace = redemption.

Questions to Discuss with the Pastor and CCM Team

Whom would you contact regarding ethical issues?

Do you understand the legalities of pastoral responsibility?

What are your clear pastoral boundaries?

How do you make it clear to a congregant what those boundaries are?

Is your office furniture set up to create a space that maintains boundaries?

Is there a window in your door?

Do you know what types of behaviors must be reported to the authorities?

- To church authorities?

- To law enforcement agencies and child- and elder-care protective agencies?

- Do you know what steps to take to make a report?

Have you ever used a personal counselor during especially stressful seasons?

Can you debrief with fellow clergy?

Is there someone to whom you are not related or a confidant in whom you can confide?

When have you experienced redemption as a result of rules and grace together?

Have you seen redemption happen with only grace or with only rules?

Key to a healing ministry is an understanding of appropriate boundaries that model a deep sense of respect for our care receiver as we help provide a greater connection to God.

DEVELOPING GOOD BOUNDARIES

- Be aware of your emotions and role as the pastor/CCM.

- Take caution in sharing personal information.

- Consider carefully touch, posture, and tone of voice.

- Understand place and time to do visits.

- Consider the importance of confidentiality while maintaining documentation and debriefing.

- Listen, reflect, comfort, and support with spiritual guidance.

- Practice extra caution with critical situations.

Assessing Your Community

As you finish this chapter, take time to consider these four questions in the context of boundaries:

o   What is God calling you to do?

o   What are your priorities and goals?

o   Who can help you?

o   What are the ways you can accomplish each goal?

Chapter Nine

Pastoral Listening and Spiritual Guidance

Know this, my dear brothers and sisters: everyone should be quick to listen, slow to speak, and slow to grow angry.

—James 1:19

Many times, people in crisis will come first to their pastor because they hope to have a safe, confidential place to navigate a difficult situation. Remember that as you take on this role, no one is expecting you to be their savior.

Are we ready? And, I mean this seriously—are we ready spiritually to employ grace, love, and compassion? Moments of spiritual sharing can awaken and transform a person's connection to God. And in the end, that is our real goal: to connect them with God.

Just to have someone *be* with you is a gift. Giving that gift as a pastor or CCM makes a good day of ministry. Through just listening and being with someone, healing can begin to occur. This is key: the person must feel heard. This is critical to them. Convey through your tone of voice and body posture that he or she has your full attention.

A Good Listener

Visualize yourself having a conversation with someone who is a good listener. Identify characteristics that make this person a good listener. Imagine sharing with this person something going on in your life. Jot down some things you notice about your imaginary conversation with the good listener.

- o   Nonverbal communication—90 percent of what we "say" is non-verbal. Preach always and use words if you must.

- o   Verbal responses or questions.

Now, imagine an experience with *someone who isn't a good listener*. What do you remember about that encounter?

What did you learn from answering these questions that can help you develop your listening skills?

Guidelines for Listening

As a pastor or CCM, our most important job is to listen. We should prepare ourselves through prayer and meditation to enlist the help of the Spirit throughout the conversation.

Pray about the upcoming appointment before each session. Get yourself in the right frame of mind so that God is able to work through you. Pray that your "stuff" will stay out of the way and that the light of Christ might shine in you, and flow out to the person seeking care.

When you begin a conversation with a congregant assure them that everything you discuss will be confidential, unless it needs to be shared with another pastor for ongoing ministry or with a psychological counselor in which case you will confer first with the congregant.

Request the congregant to sign appropriate paperwork (if needed) that pledges confidentiality about your conversation as well as paperwork regarding family contact information. Convey to them that you will be taking a few notes throughout the session. You'll find further explanation of this process, along with samples of the paperwork, in *The Congregational Care Ministry: Care Minister's Manual.*

Inform the congregant about your own ethical boundaries. As pastors and CCMs, we try to limit ourselves to four or five sessions with a congregant unless there are very unusual circumstances such as situations of grief or forgiveness that may require more sessions.

Thank the person for meeting with you. Remind the person:

- It takes courage to ask for help.

- This is a safe space to cry, if needed. Assure them you believe God works through grace and love and not judgment.

- You are honored that the person is willing to share with you.

- Make the space holy and sacred. Perhaps light a candle.

Pray with the congregant. Thank God for the opportunity to be with the person. Ask God to:

- Prepare you to hear.

- Give the person with you courage and strength to share what's on his or her heart.

- Help you be attentive to the Spirit's guidance.

Many times when I look up from the prayer, I see tears in the person's eyes, a sign of readiness to start on the healing journey.

Sample Prayer

Gracious God, we thank you for the opportunity for Jim to share what is on his heart today. Allow him to dig deep and allow me to listen with a heart that will not judge. Allow us to look together and be alert to what you might be adding to this conversation. All this we pray in your Son's healing name. Amen.

Examples of Helpful Questions

Beginning Questions

- What brings you here today? What's on your heart today?
- If this is not the first visit, you might review your previous session and then ask what has transpired since you last met.

Clarifying Questions

- Could you tell me more about that?
- How did that make you feel?

Spiritual Questions

- How is it with your soul?
- What is your relationship with God?
- When did you feel closest to God?
- Listen to clues about the person's spiritual well-being, including prayer life, reading scripture, journaling, quiet moments, activity in groups, and worship.
- Are you connecting with God on a daily or weekly basis?

Questions When You Are Caring for Couples with Marital Problems

- Do you both want this marriage to work?
- Do you pray and worship together?

Questions When You See Signs of Depression or Mental Illness That Alarm You

o How are you sleeping? How are you eating?

o Have you ever felt suicidal? Do you have a plan to harm yourself?

o If there is anything that makes you think the person is suicidal or might harm someone else, share that you are obligated by law to share the information with the appropriate people. All helping professionals are required to report child abuse. Your reporting requirements as well as the limits of confidentiality may vary according to your state laws. Please make sure you know these regulations and can communicate them as needed to persons seeking care.

Questions When You Are Caring for Someone in Relationship Crisis

o Are you in a safe place right now?

o Do you have a plan if you need to get out quickly?

Authentic Listening

This may seem like an easy task, but authentic listening takes skill and patience. Skilled listeners know how to ask leading questions and make reflective statements that will help the person open up. Important ideas for listening include:

o paying attention,

o paraphrasing or restating what the person shared,

o reiterating the feelings described,

o asking open-ended questions that require a response other than yes or no, and

o being sensitive to clues that identify:

- harmful situations where anger or sexuality issues may be a risk. If you see something, say something.

- family systems that you need to uncover.

- a family history that bears out certain repeated behaviors.

- whether the person always tries to manage everything.

Other Key Tips for Listening

Be Prepared

o Mentally

- Clear your thoughts.

- Do not try to think of answers ahead of time.

- Be a non-anxious presence.

o Physically

- Sit facing the person.

- Make eye contact.

- Lean forward.

- Have materials you need with you (pen, paper, Bible, tissue, forms to sign).

- Remind the person this is a safe place if she or he seems hesitant to share.

- Eliminate distractions—no cell phones, loud noises, or people chatting outside your door.

- Allow her or him to speak without interruption.

- Be attentive; no yawning. Don't look around the room.

- Listen to how something is said.

- Observe the person's body language and what might be left unsaid.

Be Empathetic

o   Allow the person to express his or her emotions.

o   Acknowledge the person's pain, fear, anxiety, sadness.

o   Sitting in silence can be a gift.

o   Do not make assumptions.

o   Offer feedback but resist giving advice.

o   Repeat or paraphrase what is shared.

It is helpful to recognize three levels of listening:

1. Internal listening where we are thinking about our daily activities, lists, and so forth.

2. Focused listening where we are listening intently to the other person.

3. Higher spiritual listening where we are aware of God's guidance throughout the conversation.

As you listen, be aware of your own feelings. Do not share these with the person seeking help. Your feelings are a clear signal about what is actually happening in the room. For example, if you typically find yourself feeling totally or unusually drained after meeting with a particular person, this may indicate how others also respond to him or her. You may have conversations that are very draining. Also, your feelings may also indicate or be related to how empty that person feels.

Another example: If you find yourself feeling bored or as if the person really is not talking to you, but to someone else, this may indicate that deeper psychological issues may need to be addressed by a more seasoned counselor. Consult with a respected and trusted colleague. Allowing people to feel what they are feeling is important. Just having a safe place to express your feelings is a luxury. Sometimes as humans, we know that our feelings are shortsighted or contrary to what we would like them to be. What a gift it is to have someone simply acknowledge our humanness and wait patiently with us through our processing. As people speak the words to describe their feelings, they hear themselves and begin to move in a different direction.

Wait

o   Wait for them to begin to reveal to you where they see the situation going.

o   Help people consider how to live in chaos or wait until the right solution is seen clearly. This is one of the hardest things to do.

o   People usually want some sort of immediate direction. Usually, I find they already know the direction they should go; they just want you to affirm it or call it into question.

Reflect

After the story has been told, allow time to reflect briefly on what you have heard.

o   Do your best not to issue judgmental statements; let grace work.

o   Allow the person to see mercy in your thinking so that they might model it.

o   Sometimes you cannot find adequate words in response to the person's story. It is OK to simply say, "Wow, I'm finding it hard to find words. Your situation is so difficult." This is rare, but when you think you have heard it all, someone will retell a story of a traumatic death or childhood abuse. When you hear such stories for the first time, you may feel completely unequipped to help. At such moments, seek out mentors or trusted confidants who can help you debrief and guide you for the next session.

o   A pastoral response is just that: pastoral. It can include the use of scripture, prayer, teaching, or reflective thinking. It is not clinical; there's a big difference. One helpful question (when appropriate) is "Who do you identify with in the scriptures?"

o   If there are theological questions, I try to give biblical backup to my answers. (See the end of this chapter for suggested scripture passages.) I might suggest books that I have found helpful for the situations. I keep a short list of books on the subjects of grief, marriage, sexual abuse, addiction, and so forth. (See the recommended reading list of useful books at the back of this text.)

Homework

Homework helps. Always try to give the individual, couple, or family some homework. It might be memorizing a certain scripture, attending worship, getting into a support group, going out on a date, creating a collage that tells their family story, or taking care of themselves in concrete ways. Keep a record of any scripture, book, or other homework that you assign during the session so you can remember to ask about it at the next meeting. (Document in your pastor care notes.)

Next Steps

o   Set goals.

o   Ask the person to spend time in self-reflection:

    –   What is good in their life?

    –   What brings them joy?

    –   How would any changes help their life?

o   Contact a certified counselor, if needed.

Spiritual Guidance

o   Make scriptural suggestions.

o   Suggest ways to grow through prayer, journaling, meditation, saying the "Serenity Prayer," daily devotions, breath prayer, *lectio divina*, and so on.

o   Encourage new daily spiritual disciplines (twenty-one days makes a habit).

o   Remind the person that action precedes emotion.

o   Help them take small steps and to be patient with themselves.

o   Ask if they would like to talk to someone who has gone through this situation.

o   Direct them to classes that may help them through their grief, parenting, or relationships issues.

Support

o   Ask if there are family members or friends the congregant trusts and can call.

o   Encourage good boundaries by telling those you are helping when it would be appropriate to call you, another CCM, or pastor.

Accountability

o   Email/call the CCM, pastor, or someone else to tell how the person is doing.

o   Is the person willing to meet with someone weekly?

Use the Spiritual Care Assessment Form to track each session. This will help you maintain a record of spiritual issues presented by the person, spiritual components of a spiritual care plan/intervention, and spiritual outcomes of the plan/intervention. You'll find this form in *The Congregational Care Ministry: Care Minister's Manual.*

Case Studies

Working in threes, role-play a listening session. One person is seeking care, another is a caregiver, and the third serves as evaluator. Possible scenarios include:

o   young woman hospitalized with abdominal pain,

o   sixty-five-year-old man whose wife has died,

o   person with chronic financial problems, and

o   teenager alleging sexual abuse by a teacher.

Crisis

When there is a crisis, the person needs concrete next steps for at least a week. Ask the person, "When you leave today, what will you do when _____?" In the next seven days, have the person identify:

o   a planned activity—preferably with someone,

o   someone to call every day if he or she has trouble (a different person each day if possible),

o   emergency contact information, and

o   when they will attend church two times this week (either virtually or in person)—once in worship and once in another activity.

During the next week, have the person plan two or three steps similar to those for the previous seven days. Have the person identify what to do if he or she struggles. For example:

o   List what brings the person life—going for a walk, reading a book, and so on. Have a list ready.

o   Prepare a list of people who have been through what the person is going through. Even if you don't connect these people, you have a new resource.

LGBTQIA+ Ministry

One of the gifts of our current society is a greater curiosity and openness to helping people understand their sexual identity. A good day of ministry is to have someone trust us enough to share their questions and struggles in this regard. Although pastors and CCMs are not scientists, sociologists, or psychological counselors, we can offer important assurances, encouragement, and spiritual guidance regarding God's gift of creating each person unique and special in their own way. It has been proven over and again that people who are not accepted by their faith communities are much more inclined toward anxiety, depression, and suicide. Let us be a community of faith for all people where everyone is seen as a child of God. n that regard, there are a few important ideas to consider:

1. Educate yourself and your care team through books and knowledgeable speakers about the sexual spectrum.

2. Bring in speakers to help you and others know how to speak with greater sensitivity, eliminating hurtful phrases or words.

3. Create small groups that identify as LGBTQIA+ with non-judgmental facilitators.

4. Include LGBTQIA+ individuals on your care team and other leadership opportunities in your church.

5. Be ready to assure congregants of God's love and grace. If they have been rejected by their families of origin, assure them that the church family is there for them.

6. Invite them to visit with someone in the church who has gone through their own process of coming out who can help them name their fears and anxieties.

7. Know which counselors in your community could provide supportive care.

8. If a person shows signs of hurting themselves make sure you offer immediate next steps with counseling or medical professionals.

9. Assign CCMs who will check in on these persons regularly for as long as needed.

10. Have on hand encouraging books such as Adam Hamilton's *Making Sense of the Bible.* This text will help the person process the confusing scriptures as well as give them uplifting scriptures, such as 1 Corinthians 13 and 1 John 4.

Personal Encouragement from Karen

When I was first appointed to the United Methodist Church of the Resurrection in 2003, our son, Paul, was just starting his senior year in high school. In September he came out to his classmates and sisters. A few days later he came out to my husband and me. This information was both startling and made us fearful for Paul.

How would he be accepted throughout his life? Would he be persecuted and taunted? We did our best to offer him nonjudgmental support through counseling as well as guidance through other pastors in our area. He received it well. I truly believe that the church's acceptance in this regard helped Paul immensely as he came to peace with himself over the years since then.

What I know from this is that even though we all are not in agreement regarding LGBTQIA+ full inclusion into the church, this is a matter of life and death. My prayers for our greater growth as people of faith is that we will be a relevant church unafraid and nonjudgmental to offer the love and grace of God.

Please note the recommended reading lists at the back of the book.

Some Sessions Are Difficult

Some sessions offer surprising challenges. People can become frustrated or start digging into things that are hurtful or scary as they remember them. Try your best to remain a listening presence, but do not allow their emotions to pull you into extra drama. A skilled pastor or CCM realizes that most people aren't even aware of the mechanisms they use to cope. Many times, I have seen people go from being calm to tearful to angry within seconds. It is as if from childhood they learned that this is how to get their way or get their points advanced. Be alert for any patterns of manipulation. Help people grow by showing them other ways of communicating.

Be Alert

Be ever vigilant of the dangers of wading into deeper waters where you don't have the skill level to be helpful. (More detailed information and training are included in chapter 14, "Mental Health Ministry.") Three quick points to remember:

o   Seek psychological counseling for the person when you see it is needed.

o   There have been occasions during appointments in my office when a person has been suicidal, necessitating me to take immediate action with the person's family or other community/church professionals.

o   Keep a list of phone numbers of places and persons in your community that provide mental health and suicide-prevention help.

o   If you sense danger of self-harm or of harming others, do not hesitate to call 911. There have been times when I have been on the phone with someone who was suicidal and I have had another person call 911.

The congregant may be frustrated with you, but they will also appreciate that you were trying to do everything you could to help, particularly when it may have meant life or death. Again, remember that there are legal reporting requirements.

A safety and self-care contract is a good tool for these difficult situations. This form can be useful in adding accountability or in slowing down or interrupting emotional responses. When both of you sign this document, a course of action becomes real. Your signature is also a tangible sign to the congregant that you care about his or her well-being. You'll find a sample of this contract in *The Congregational Care Ministry: Care Minister's Manual.*

Offer Comfort

The scriptures tell us, "Comfort, comfort my people!" (Isaiah 40:1). Always offer a next step for those who come to see you, even if it is just seeing them in worship next week. They have come to you, spilled their story, and offered you a part of their life that perhaps no one else has ever heard. You are acting on behalf of Christ and the church. What would Christ do for this lamb? One prayer tool you can share is a simple ABC Prayer:

A = *acknowledging* how you are feeling, without judgment.

B = *being aware* of your breath. Breathing in peace, exhale your pain.

C = *choosing to* be full of love, light, grace, peace, and joy.

Assessing Your Community

o   Whom do you consider a good listener?

o   What is your prayer routine before, during, and after meeting with a person seeking care?

o   Using the listening guidelines in this chapter, evaluate your listening skills.

  –   What is working well?

  –   What needs improvement?

Chapter Ten

Visitation

If any of you are suffering, they should pray.

—James 5:13

Hospital visitation is one of the most important elements of care that can be offered through the church. As a pastor or CCM, you serve with skilled eyes and an intuitive heart, understanding the multiple dimensions of being human that are closely intertwined. When the body is distressed, spiritual and psychological well-being also can be affected. Be sensitive to the implications of physical change or pain. It is a complex ministry and must be bathed with prayer. Also important to note up front is the need to attend to the family of the sick. When a person is hurting, family and friends may need care too.

All the information in this section will help the patient know that you and the church are going to be walking beside him or her during this hospitalization.

If you have ever been hospitalized or have had surgery, you will understand that this is a sacred time for individuals and their families. You are allowed to see and be with people at vulnerable moments. Cherish this time. It is precious. Hospital visitation is a complex ministry and must be bathed with prayer.

How Hospital Visitation Works

Because of the complexity of demands upon any pastor or pastoral staff, care can best be accomplished through a team effort. Similar to the specific areas of care a medical team observes, it is important to educate the congregation and care team to follow clear lines of care while applying best practices.

Gathering Information

o   The congregation must contact the church to request care for people who are sick. The three usual methods are:

  –   calling the church office,

  –   submitting prayer request cards, which are usually received in the offering plates during worship services or electronically, and

  –   contacting through a pager, which can be rotated among pastoral staff and CCMs.

o   All requests for care go to one central place or person on staff, who then triages the intake and deploys the caregivers. This person's position is extremely important, be it staff person or volunteer, because of the volume of care that is needed at any church.

o   Communicate clearly to your congregation their responsibility to get information to the church. In turn, communication to the congregation can be conveyed through the pulpit, bulletin, or weekly church emails. You cannot visit if you do not know someone is sick or injured!

o   The triage person finds out the hospital or surgical date, time, and place as well as the patient's relationship to the church.

o   The triage person also gathers names and contact information for friends and family and the reason for admission (if the patient wants that information given out).

o This information is stored electronically and handwritten on a central calendar. It can also be posted on a calendar white board seen *only* by pastoral staff and CCMs.

Emergency Guidelines

o If the patient has been admitted unexpectedly, visit within twenty-four hours of receiving information.

o If the request is for emergency care, a pastor is notified so an immediate visit can happen quickly.

o If the pastor cannot go, a key CCM is deployed based on the location of the hospital. Those who live or work closest to the hospital will be asked to make the initial visit.

o This procedure is for the weekday routine, but over a weekend, it is important to give your congregation a way they can access care. The usual means are through a cell phone or pager contact that is listed publicly, for example, in the Sunday bulletin.

o Gather contact information for the patient and family or friends.

Follow Up after Initial Visit

o Document the visit, including information gathered about the illness, who was present, and the care given (anointing, scripture reading, and prayer).

o Suggest a plan for follow-up care.

o Give this information to the triage person, who can create the follow-up care plan.

o The pastor should always be informed of important changes in the patient's care and condition.

o Let the family or individual know what the next steps will be in your caregiving.

Caregiving Guidelines for Special Situations

o   If the patient is a child, a volunteer or pastoral staff makes a daily contact. The pastor sets a personal standard of visiting at least two times a week.

o   If the patient is in intensive care or in critical condition, the pastor or CCM visits every day.

o   If death is imminent, the pastor visits and assesses the situation to determine caregiving.

o   If the patient has a prolonged illness, the CCM provides follow-up care as the pastor assigns.

o   If the patient is dying or has died, this is of utmost concern and urgency. When death occurs, the pastor is to be notified ASAP, and then go immediately to the family. If the church office is notified by a pager call, the pastor on call or a CCM is to *go immediately* to be with the family.

Protocol for Hospital Calls

o   Begin with the basics. Learn where to park at the hospital(s) in your community.

o   Dress appropriately. Wear washable clothing for hospital calls. Stay safe, and gown up if necessary.

o   Make sure you have your "hospital kit" with you.

   –   your Bible (I keep one in the car.)
   –   anointing oil
   –   business cards
   –   small supply of appropriate gifts
      • prayer shawls
      • lap quilts
      • small Bible with special verses marked
      • small devotional book

- Name tag
  - Be sure to wear your name tag so that your intentions are clear to hospital staff, the patient you are visiting, and family members. Your name tag will also be helpful if the family or staff do not know your name.
  - If surgery is planned, call the day prior to verify information.

o Pray for your ministry before you arrive. A good rule of thumb is to arrive before the patient's scheduled check-in time. If you wait too long, you may lose your opportunity to pray with the person and their family.

o Check in at the reception desk or nurses' station and request to pray with the patient. You may need to wait until you (and possibly the family) are called into the pre-op room.

o When you enter the room, introduce yourself to the patient and the family.

o Be aware of hospital staff needs.

o Read scripture, anoint, and pray. (See Anointing Service and Suggested Scriptures at the end of this chapter.) It is probably best not to use the Twenty-Third Psalm unless requested or it is a near-death situation.

o Offer the family appropriate contact information to call, text, or email updates. Appropriate follow-up is essential.

o Obtain the person and family's contact information, if appropriate.

o Excuse yourself.

o Pray outside the room.

Protocol for a Nonsurgical Hospital Visit

o Pray before you enter the room.

o Identify comforting and appropriate scripture in advance.

o Wear gown and gloves, if needed. Be careful not to put yourself at risk of being contaminated.

o Knock. Say, "This is _____ from the church. Is now a good time for me to visit?"

   - If yes, walk in and introduce yourself to the patient and family members.

   - If no, respect their privacy and pray silently outside the door.

   - If the person is asleep or away for tests or therapy, pray silently and leave a note saying you visited.

o Explain your connection to the church.

o If there are others in the room, ask their relationship to the patient.

o Sit at eye level with the patient, but not on the bed. Ask for permission to sit in a chair if one is close by. In the hospital, people feel powerless. Asking for permission empowers them and assures them of your sensitivity to their situation.

o Ask how he or she is doing today.

   - If you do not know the reason for the hospitalization, ask.

   - Other questions may include: How have you been sleeping? Is there anything or anyone you'd like for us to offer prayer for today? How are your friends and family doing with your hospitalization? How is it with your soul?

   - If you have known the person for a while, it may be comforting to recall memories of more normal times together.

o Speak clearly, calmly, and gently.

   - Speak to the patient, even if he or she is in a coma. He or she can hear you.

   - It's OK to touch patients, appropriately and gently.

o Listen to the person's story. Ask open-ended questions that relate to the person's needs.

o Do not relate your own personal story of suffering or talk about someone else with the same illness, operation, or injury.

o Help the patient remember his or her faith and that God loves and is with him or her.

   – It may surprise you to learn that many patients feel that God has abandoned them or is punishing them for some wrongdoing.

   – Remind the patient of the hope and healing that God wants for him or her and of God's steadfast concern for his or her well-being.

o *Keep your visit brief,* respect privacy and the need for rest.

o Tell the patient you would like to pray for them. Ask, "What would you like me to pray for you?" Let them explain fully.

o Read an appropriate scripture.

o Ask the patient if you can anoint him or her before you pray if this has not been done in prior visits. Remind those present that the scriptures tell us to anoint as we pray for healing. James 5:14 says, "If any of you are sick, they should call for the elders of the church, and the elders should pray over them, anointing them with oil in the name of the Lord."

o Conclude your visit with a prayer of assurance, strength, and healing.

o Thank the patient for allowing you to visit and let him or her know when to expect the next visit.

o Give the patient or the family your business card. Let all of them know that they can call the church if any other care is needed.

o Let the patient and family know when they can expect another visit from the church and who might be coming.

Other Considerations

o   If there is a patient in another bed in the room, respect his or her privacy and need for rest. Keep your voice low.

o   Do not assist with transfers from or to bed. Get help.

o   Become familiar with hospital terminology.

o   Do not visit if *you* are sick.

o   Be careful not to cross-contaminate in your visiting. Wash your hands between visits. As you enter a room, use alcohol sanitizer, if available. Wear a mask when appropriate.

o   Carefully plan the order of your visits. If someone is infectious, do not visit him or her *before* seeing someone else who is post-op.

o   Remember your shoes also can carry germs from one room to another.

Caring for People Who Are Frail

Frailty is a journey of spiritual, physical, social, cognitive, sensory, or mobility challenges that can combine in many different ways to cause loss of strength and decreased activity.

o   It may begin with a fall.

o   It may happen slowly.

o   No two people follow the same path.

Caring for people who are frail is a gift of your time and presence to people who are unable to attend church. It reminds them that others care about them and that they are remembered. It allows people who are frail to continue growing in faith in this season of their lives.

Levels of Care

o Independent living—people are reasonably able to meet activities of daily living (eating, moving about, toileting, bathing, and dressing).

o Assisted living—people need more help with daily living activities. They may have dementia or be confused.

o Skilled nursing—people have a great need for assistance.

o Some people can stay at home safely.

o Some people need to be in a facility better equipped to help care for them.

o Some people will fall into these three categories at different times.

Who Provides Care to People Who Are Frail?

o Pastor provides care on a regular basis to develop a relationship for ongoing care. However, it would be unrealistic for the pastor to do all the visiting.

o Laity or CCMs who have spiritual gifts of compassion and mercy can provide care. Serving in this way blesses both the caregiver and the frail.

o A best practice is to provide continuity of care by having the same CCM visit the person in need. That way, the congregant and her or his family will begin to relate to the CCM. It is also a good practice to have the same team of volunteers visit the same facility so that they can get to know staff.

How Often?

Establish a schedule with realistic expectations about frequency. Visits can be monthly or weekly, depending on circumstances, but they need to be continuous, consistent, and reliable.

Be flexible if the person's health deteriorates. Between visits, make phone calls, send emails (if that is acceptable to the congregant), or write a note.

Boundaries

When visiting a person who is frail, observe the basic boundaries listed in chapter 9 as you balance grace with discipline. Here are some specific guidelines to follow when visiting a person who is frail.

In a Nursing Home or Assisted Living Facility

o   Let the nursing staff know you are visiting and when you leave, particularly if the congregant is in a private room or does not have a roommate.

o   Try to meet together in common areas or keep the door to the room open.

o   Keep track of the person if he or she moves to another room or facility.

o   Limit your visit to five minutes in a nursing home and ten minutes in an assisted living facility.

Home Visit

o   Let someone else know when you will visit. You may need to visit in teams due to the complete privacy of a home visit.

o   Men visit men; women visit women.

Touching/Hugging

o   Appropriate touching includes holding a hand or gently touching a forearm, shoulder, or back. This can be a blessing and demonstrate to the congregant that you care.

o   Touching or hugging must be done carefully and respectfully. Always ask permission.

o   Be aware of any needs to social distance.

Other Guidelines for Communicating with People Who Are Frail

Before you enter the room, pray for the Lord to guide your words and increase your receptiveness. Pray that your words will be understood and that the person will be blessed by your visit. Pause and assess the person's level of care. Are they walking without assistance? Are they using a walker? Are they in a wheelchair?

Be Seen and Heard

o Always approach the person from the front.

o Be on the same eye level (sitting or standing) as the person you are visiting. Kneel or sit in a chair next to him or her.

o Speak and move slowly.

o Let the person know who you are, even if you have visited before.

 - Wear your name tag.

 - Listen, listen, listen.

 - Don't hurry.

 - Don't discount the person if he or she doesn't make sense.

 - Don't talk for the person, interrupt him or her, or talk about the person as if he or she isn't there.

Communicating with a Person Who Is Confused

o If the person is not oriented to time and place and may not be in the same reality that you are, go to where he or she is. For example, the person may talk about a baby sleeping in the next room.

o Enter the person's world and share it.

o Do not argue; it is unlikely you will win!

o Redirect by asking questions that use specific sights, smells, or sounds. For example, ask, "Did your mother bake bread?"

o   Ask about things the person does remember.

o   Speak in simple sentences that express one idea or subject at a time.

o   If the person becomes agitated, end the conversation with prayer and return another day.

Developing a Relationship with a Person Who Is Frail

o   Try to help the person review his or her life. Write down the person's stories.

o   Pray the Lord's Prayer and a prayer of forgiveness.

o   Use familiar scriptures.

o   Offer anointing and Communion.

–   If the person has swallowing problems, break the wafer into quarters and dip it into the juice.

–   If the person has dementia, hold the elements in the person's line of vision and ask if he or she would like to receive Communion.

o   Bring with you copies of sermons or the church bulletin, large-print devotionals, and Communion elements and anointing oil.

o   Leave a note for the family or call them to let them know you visited. Ask the family to contact you if the person's situation changes, and include your contact information in the note. Include the date of your next visit.

PRACTICE: ROLE-PLAY VISITING SOMEONE WHO IS FRAIL

Work in threes to role-play visiting someone who is frail and in a nursing home. One person is frail, another person is providing care, and the third person is the observer.

Using the guidelines for visiting people who are frail, role-play for three minutes the caregiver communicating with the nursing home resident, who is in a wheelchair and is hard of hearing.

- What did the caregiver do before visiting the person who is frail?
- How did the caregiver approach the frail person?
- How did the caregiver react to the frail person's being in a different reality?
- How did the caregiver speak? How did the frail person react?
- How did the caregiver engage the frail person in conversation?
- What did the caregiver do before leaving?

If there is time, change roles and repeat.

Special Elements and Situations

Communion

Communion is an amazing gift to those who are in vulnerable health situations. As pastors, be sure you have the elements prepared and ready for your CCMs to take with them on their visits. Some details to remember for Communion include:

o   Have fresh juice and bread that has been consecrated by a pastor.

o   Prepare the table with great respect.

o   You can purchase a small Communion set for such situations or use prepackaged juice and wafers.

o   Put a small, clean cloth under the elements as you set them up on the bedside table.

o   Make it a sacred space for the sacrament you are making available.

o   If the patient is unable to ingest the elements, ask the nurse for a mouth swab to dab the juice on the tongue. Break off a tiny piece of bread for a small taste.

o   Always make sure you have washed your hands before and after serving Communion.

Baptism

o   Pastors may want to connect with a hospital chaplain for help with set up. At the very least be prepared with a small bowl for water.

o   Have anointing oil to anoint for healing.

o   If the person to be baptized is a child who may not live, be sure you are prepared to ask appropriate questions of the parents and family. It will not be the usual, "Will you promise to raise this child in the body of believers?" Be prepared to say something like this: "Will you promise to love and nurture this child that he or she might understand the love of God through your care?" (Again, check with a hospital chaplain about sensitive language in this regard.)

o   If the child lives, the family will raise him or her in the body of believers. If the child dies, the family will feel good about their promise to love the child as any devoted Christian parent would.

o   The key here is to be very sensitive and very *prepared.*

Ask for Assistance

Many pastors and CCMs feel at home and at ease in a hospital or nursing home setting. If you do not, you may need to find ways to overcome your fears and aversion. I encourage you to keep trying, as I truly believe this is one of the most sacred places for a pastor or volunteer to be. Life-and-death issues are common. Incredible ministry is possible in this setting.

o   Be patient with yourself.

o   Usually, you will find that over time the sights, sounds, smells, hallways, and rooms become more familiar and thus lose their fright factor.

o   If a situation is critical and you must do ministry in an emergency room with family and friends, take along a colleague to help or contact the hospital chaplain (if available) ahead of time.

o   As you practice this ministry in a geographic region, you will get to know the hospital chaplains who can help you understand the situation you are about to encounter.

o   Many hospitals also have special places to speak with family members privately and some have chapels that are open for prayer and even worship services.

Redemption Story 6: Lisa's Story, Part 1

The page came on a Sunday regarding the illness of Lisa, a middle-aged wife and mother of three adolescent children. The day before, Lisa experienced a seizure and lost consciousness. When Lisa, who was also a pediatric nurse practitioner, came to, she quickly realized that she needed help. She was hospitalized and an MRI showed frightening results: a glioblastoma brain tumor.

This was all I knew when I walked into the hospital room full of family. I remember meeting her mother and father, husband, sister, and three children. We all sensed hanging in the room the question, "What next?"

On that first visit, Lisa seemed relieved and glad to see someone from church; her mother and father did too. For the others, although they welcomed me, I saw fear in their eyes. They told me that there would be more tests in the next few days to discover the type of cancer. That afternoon, we read scriptures to help calm the anxiety (for example, 1 Peter 5:7-11); then I anointed Lisa and prayed for complete healing and relief from pain. How does redemption or restoration happen through such a situation?

Follow-Up Care

Contact the person one or two days after they have arrived home. This can be done through a phone call, text, email or written note. If they are facing a challenging long term health situation discuss with the person how and when they would like to receive care.

Documentation

After every visit the CCM, volunteer, and pastor should document in whatever way has been created for confidential storing of the information. Many churches prefer to use an electronic spreadsheet that will help them keep track of the person's health situation and the care given. Others will rely on notebooks and an alphabetized system of documentation. Some are able to store the information in their church's database in very confidential links that are only accessible to pastors and CCMs. Whatever means you have, it is important to emphasize that documentation will help you remember who has done the care, what scriptures the person used, who was present at the visit, the patient's condition, and so forth.

Anointing Service

In the Christian tradition, anointing with oil offers an opportunity for spiritual healing, affirmed by scripture in James 5:13-15. This prayer of faith says, "If any of you are suffering, they should pray. If any of you are happy, they should sing. If any of you are sick, they should call for the elders of the church, and the elders should pray over them, anointing them with oil in the name of the Lord. Prayer that comes from faith will heal the sick, for the Lord will restore them to health. And if they have sinned, they will be forgiven."

One book of worship notes, "Anointing the forehead with oil is a sign invoking the healing love of God. The oil points to beyond itself and those doing the anointing to the action of the Holy Spirit and the presence of the healing Christ, who is God's Anointed One."[1]

Anointing gives the opportunity for spiritual healing, which is a wholeness of body, mind, and spirit. Anointing offers healing, rather than a cure. Anointing people is a powerful reminder of God's triune presence in their journey, offering the peace that they do not travel alone. If they are near the end of life, anointing helps complete their circle of faith.

How It Works

o   After ample sharing has occurred, tell the person you would like to pray for him or her.

o   Ask, "What would you like me to pray?" Let him or her explain fully.

o   Ask if you may anoint him or her before you pray.

o   The person may not be familiar with anointing. Explain anointing and what it represents. Ask the person if he or she wants to experience this.

o   Read James 5:13-15.

o   Secure the person's permission or the permission of the family present in the room.

o Explain that you will put oil on your thumb and then make the sign of the cross on the forehead.

o Remind them that this is not offered as a cure but as an invitation to the Holy Spirit to be present with them, offering wholeness in the love of Christ.

o Put oil on your thumb. As you make the sign of the cross on the person's forehead, say, "I anoint you with oil in the name of the Father, Son, and Holy Spirit."

o Pray for complete healing and the release of any fears or anxieties the person may have.

o Pray the Lord's Prayer together.

Read Psalm 23, reminding them that God walks with them through all the valleys, even those as dark as death. Tip: Insert the person's name in place of the first-person personal pronouns in Psalm 23. For example, "You, Lord, are _____'s shepherd. _____ will never be in need. You let _____ rest in fields of green grass. You lead _____ to streams of peaceful water and you refresh_____'s life."

Suggested Scriptures

o Psalm 19:14

o Psalm 23

o Psalm 34:4

o Psalm 106:1

o Psalm 145:18

o Proverbs 3:5-6

o Isaiah 43:1-5

o John 14:1-6

o Romans 12:12

o   Romans 8:26-27

o   Romans 8:38-39

o   Ephesians 3:20-21

o   Philippians 4:6-7

o   Colossians 4:2

o   1 John 5:14-15

o   James 1:5-6

o   Hebrews 12:14-15

o   1 Peter 5:6-10

o   Revelation 21:1-5

Assessing Your Community

Readiness is essential in making visitations. With your table group or small group, discuss your protocol for visiting people who are in the hospital.

o   What communication channels are available to alert you to a person who seeks care in the hospital?

o   What is your protocol for visiting a person before surgery? After surgery?

o   What is your protocol for visiting a person who is infectious?

o   If you have many hospitals in your community, how do you arrange visits?

o   If your hospital is in another community, how do you arrange visits?

o   What have you learned from one another or in this chapter about making hospital visits?

Chapter Eleven

Leading through the Darkest Valley

Even when I walk through the darkest valley,
I fear no danger because you are with me.

—Psalm 23:4

You only bury your mother once. Heaven forbid that you would have to bury your child. Yet, when you are a pastor or CCM, you will lead people through these events many times. I am convinced that there is no greater service that you can give a family than to lead them through this valley. In fact, I believe that death supersedes every other element of pastoral ministry. It is the greatest fear that most people face. But, it is the gift of Jesus's life, death, and resurrection that he conquered the grave: *"Where is your victory, Death? / Where is your sting?"* (1 Corinthians 15:55).

As you lead people through this valley, you will discover that moments of redemption can happen in many ways.

o   As people gather, the petty grievances can disappear if you provide good leadership.

o   You can actually help dysfunctional families if they are open to your help.

o   I have seen relationships restored over and over again.

Christ came to make these moments of redemption possible. When you come to minister during these difficult times, you help people experience these moments for themselves as individuals and sometimes as a community.

Commit to the Journey

Death can be a downward spiral with twists and turns. Your care will be ongoing and consistent, honoring and meeting the person where he or she is.

Death should take priority over every other ministry situation or meeting you may be doing. Go to the family; don't just make a phone call. Do not assume a brief prayer over the phone will be adequate. You must *go*. You represent the presence of Christ. No matter what the age or circumstances of the deceased, the family feels an immense loss.

What if you are the last person who visits to represent Christ and the church? The dying and their family are blessed by the presence of the church—even when they cannot communicate. The family is looking to you to provide prayer, scriptures of God's promises, and words of comfort. The sacred moments around a body can be especially important for the family. This is a moment when their hope in Christ is affirmed. Jesus must show up.

During a time of pandemic or extraordinary circumstances when you cannot physically be present, do not take on shame or guilt but rather give yourself grace as you extend Christ's love through the phone or whatever means of communication that you have. Pastors and CCMs can carry a heavy load in this way and during challenging times we must encourage one another and remember that we are a team that can help carry the load.

It is also an important step to train your congregation regarding what the church will offer during the dying process and the eventual death. This can be done through classes or sermons. Then as a person approaches death they will find comfort in your communication whether it be at the bedside or via phone or email. This process will help them release their fears regarding death.

Long Journey

If the prognosis is for a long journey toward death, create a team of people who can attend to the person.

Create a patient time line of important events ahead. Chemotherapy? How often? Surgery? Ask the person if there are people he or she is concerned about or tasks that need to be completed. Are there people with whom the person needs to make peace? Is there a funeral plan in place? Does the person have a living will (do-not-resuscitate document, medical and durable power of attorney)?

Sometimes people do not know how to articulate these questions. You can help by introducing the person and the family to Caring Conversations, a booklet that can be accessed online (https://www.practicalbioethics.org/resources/caring-conversations.html). Another tool that is helpful for these conversations is a Spiritual Autobiography that helps them think through their funeral plans, any unfinished business, and what they consider to be their legacy. An example of such a document can be found in *The Caring Congregation Ministry: Care Minister's Manual.*

Palliative and Hospice Care

When an individual or family approaches the time when either it is clear that life cannot be sustained nor is there any medical intervention that can provide quality of life, he or she, along with family members, may make an intentional choice for palliative or hospice care. Many people fear even the word *hospice*, so shifting that fear to gratitude can be a part of the pastoral ministry. Good palliative and eventually hospice care will provide the family with a journey that is sacred and helpful for the individual dying.

Many times, the term "palliative support" is much easier for the family to accept because it assumes medical care is still happening. For instance, oxygen support may be a part of the care. Some families worry that even saying the word *hospice* around the terminally ill person will give the impression that the family has given up and thus hastens the loved one's death. Doctors and nurses who work with this situation can be so helpful as you work together to mitigate the fear that the family is experiencing. Trusted pastors and CCMs can be very helpful in this regard especially if these conversations begin before the time that the end-of-life care is needed.

At some point, hopefully, the family will begin to understand that hospice care can offer greater assistance, which can include bathing and medical equipment that can be very helpful for the daily care of the patient. The actual dying process can take months, thus it is very draining for the family. Some people actually go off hospice if they are getting better.

One important medical note: research has shown that forcing the dying person to eat causes him or her more pain, since the organs naturally trying to shut down are forced to work. This is an important concept for people to understand as they assume guilt if the person is not eating. The family may say something like, "we're starving her (or him) to death," when in actuality the loved one will experience less pain and have a much more natural end if food is not forced.

Yet, even people in the medical field may not be ready to accept that everything for their loved ones has been done. They may grasp at every possibility, even when it is not in the best interest of their loved ones. As your ministry team attends to the family, communicate among yourselves to gain understanding of where each family member is in the process.

Actively Dying

For others in hospice care, the time is short and the "actively dying" phase becomes apparent. It is important for the pastor and volunteers to commit to a plan for a daily check-in during the time when the person is actively dying.

Once the person is actively dying there may come a time when he or she is no longer responsive. Assume the person is still able to hear every word although he or she may not be able to respond or even open his or her eyes. With that in mind, talk to the person and the family as if everyone is in the conversation.

In her booklet *Gone from My Sight: The Dying Experience*, Barbara Karnes (bkbooks.com) gives the symptoms that describe the term "actively dying" by estimated time until death. They are:

o   One to three months: withdrawal from everything outside one's self, including food. Sleep increases.

o   One to two weeks before death: disorientation, sleeping most of the time.

o   Physical changes: blood pressure often lowers, the body temperature fluctuates, skin color changes, breathing changes and fluctuates.

o   One to two days to hours before death: a surge of energy; restlessness; breathing becomes slower and more irregular; congestion may sound loud; eyes open, but are not seeing; hands and feet become purplish; nonresponsive.

o   The separation becomes complete when breathing stops. Karnes writes, "What appears to be the last breath is often followed by one or two long-spaced breaths and then the physical body is empty. The owner is no longer in need of a heavy, nonfunctioning vehicle. They have entered a new city, a new life."

Unfinished Business

Ask the family if they know of any unfinished business that would help the dying person.

o   Is there anyone whom the dying person would want to hear from?

o   Is there any situation that may need resolution?

This unfinished business is such an important question for the dying person. It allows the person to make sure that situations have been resolved as best they could before death. People wait for a loved one to come to the bedside. They long to make sure all of their relationships are in a good place. This allows for that sense of "peace of God that exceeds all understanding" (Philippians 4:7).

This is what we get to do as spiritual caregivers for the dying. Could there be any higher calling?

Redemption Story 8: Brandon's Story

I was helping a young person and his family move through his death. Brandon, thirty-one, was dying of melanoma. His mom and dad were vigilant at the bedside daily. As the days passed and Brandon was no longer able to respond or even keep his eyes open, he still seemed very restless.

I asked the family if there was anything or anyone that might help Brandon; more specifically, I asked if he had any unfinished business. They talked about how Brandon's ex-wife had been texting them with words of apology, but they had not told Brandon. I asked them if they thought this would help Brandon. They prayed overnight about it and the next day read Brandon her messages. They said it seemed to offer him a sense of peace, and they could see that his restlessness subsided.

Readiness

Readiness is the key to caring for people who are dying, along with their families. Your readiness will help give them a greater chance of an amazing, sacred death experience.

o   Achieving readiness for each member of the family may take time. Be alert to where they are emotionally and spiritually.

o   Be ready to have others step in if you are absent.

o   Prepare the family for the event of death during daily visits.

o   Be ready to fully experience this journey with the family.

o   Gradually open their hearts and minds to the peace that is possible in these moments.

o   Interact calmly with any resistant member of the family, whose anger, denial, and frustration hold them back.

o   Remind them faithfully that this death is not the end.

Redemption Story 9: Lisa's Story, Part 2

Lisa used the *Caring Conversations* booklet and the spiritual autobiography to help her attend to tasks that she knew would be important. Sometimes, when she felt up to it, we had long conversations about her children, her husband, her sister, parents, and career friends. In addition, we addressed tough theological questions. My visiting Lisa brought up her concerns about God. She wanted to know, "Why me, God?"

One day Lisa called my office and asked if I could come over. It was springtime and I remember sitting outside in the family's beautiful backyard. Lisa said she was just angry that day. Although Lisa was theologically savvy and pretty much knew what answer I would give her, she just needed to step through the process to get past her anger. She had already sought answers in books I had recommended. She understood that life is not fair and that our bodies are fragile. She had been at the bedsides of children who had died. She had the "head" knowledge of life and death. But no matter who we are, we will have our moments when the questions hammer us in a profoundly personal way. It is at that moment when we need to have someone to walk through the process with us.

Confusion, anger, and hurt are allowed, but don't get stuck there. As pastors and caregivers, you wrestle with the questions and help people move forward. Some people get stuck on the "Why me?" and turn inward, becoming completely self-absorbed, pushing friends and family away. For these people, their final days can become a pity party.

One particular sacred hour that I will never forget with Lisa was when she was nearing the end of her journey. Her middle child, John, had suddenly become reluctant to go close to his mother's bed. I knelt beside her bed as she asked me to encourage John to come in and see her. John was in the living room watching television. All it took was a simple invitation: "Would you like to go with me to read some scriptures and pray with your mom?" He jumped up and said, "Sure." My hunch was that he just didn't know what to do in the space alone with her.

The twelve-year-old boy snuggled in with his mom as I knelt beside them and recited some verses of scripture in the dimly lit room. I prayed for God's holy peace and comfort to saturate the room. Then I said good-bye for the day and promised to call the next day.

This was a redeeming moment, a sacred moment of restoring the close relationship for both of them.

Lisa transferred to a nearby hospice house as her condition worsened. Daily visits were part of my routine. A CCM was also ministering to Lisa and her family. However, there was a three-day stretch when I was going to be out of town for a conference. Late one night at the conference, I received a call from Lisa's husband. He left a voice message, and I could tell from the sound of his voice that the end had come.

I called back quickly and told them I would return first thing in the morning. This meant changing my airline flight, but, at the moment, I knew Lisa's family was counting on the fact that I would show up and lead them through this. During these hours, they had to be reassured that death did not have the last word.

However, I was not able to change my flight to be at Lisa's bedside. There will be times when you simply cannot be present. Readiness must also be part of the journey, as you bring another pastor or CCM into the picture just in case you are not immediately available when the moment of death happens. One pastor stated it so clearly: "Jesus must show up." And that happens as we represent the hands, feet, voice, and presence of the living Lord.

When the Hour Is Near

When the family notifies the church that death may happen that day, go to the bedside. When you arrive at the home, hospital, or hospice, note the following:

o   When death is imminent, make sure that you communicate to the family a sense of calm and assurance about the outcome.

o   Have the family and friends circle around the bedside.

o   Begin with the idea that this is a very sacred hour. The loved one has run the race and the most important people are gathered around.

o   Speak as if that person is hearing every word you say, even if the person seems comatose.

o   As the person nears death, you, the family, and friends gather around the bed to create a bridge to heaven. This is the essence of ministry as death draws near.

o   Picture the time when the hour is near for the person who is dying.

o   The person nearing death may rally for one last word. Just assume she or he doesn't want to miss a word of what you are saying.

o   Usher in peace and calm with your presence. With our ministry of presence as well as scriptural, spiritual guidance we can help her or him have an amazing Easter experience.

o   An actual true story of how to use appropriate scripture and language is provided in this story:

Forty-nine-year-old Cheryl had been struggling for six weeks with an aortic aneurysm that could not be surgically repaired. We had CCMs and pastors visiting regularly through this challenging time. Her husband and three young adult children were attentive as were her sister and father. Her mother had died a year before also of an aortic aneurysm. Finally, her family made the decision to take her off of life support. They called me on a Saturday morning and asked if I (Karen) would come to help them though this time.

When I arrived at the hospital, the medical staff was getting ready to take her off of the ventilator. At that point I invited the family and friends into a room where we could prepare ourselves.

With everyone in the room I began to speak about how Cheryl was about to be "born into heaven." What was important at this moment was to help them get past their fear of death as they leaned into the scriptural promises of a spiritual body. For this purpose, I use portions of 2 Corinthians 4:7-18 and 5:1-7 (emphasis on verses 4:8-10, 16-18; 5:1-7a).

After reading about our heavenly bodies, I explained to the family that once the life support was turned off, Cheryl would probably live for a few minutes and we would have the opportunity to speak words of assurance to her. I invited each of the children to prepare some little thing to say to their mom to help her fly to Jesus. Most times I use the language of being a "midwife" as she is born into heaven. As those present, we are the midwives. This language gives people purpose and again helps them absorb the message of being born into a spiritual body.

As we ended our time in the family room, I prayed for "strength and assurance for each one of them" as well as "peace with no pain" for Cheryl. We then went into Cheryl's room where we encircled the bed.

At that point, assuming she could hear every word although her body was very still, I began to speak to Cheryl telling her who was around the bedside and that each one of them wanted to speak to her so she could hear their voices. One by one beginning with her husband, every person spoke words of love and gratitude to her.

As we ended that special time, I told Cheryl we were going to have some words of scripture that speak to us of eternal life as she was preparing to be born into heaven.

The first scripture was from Revelation 21:1-5 ("a new heaven and a new earth") that speaks of God making all things new. A place where "there will be no mourning, crying, or pain anymore" (v. 4). You can encourage the dying to be aware that they may begin to see people who have gone on before them in their spiritual bodies. In Cheryl's case her mother was remembered by one of the family members. For the CCM or pastor it is important to exude assurance that there is more beyond this world.

The second useful scripture is from 1 Corinthians 15:44, 50-57, which explains that "all of us won't die, but we will all be changed" (v. 51) and that the "perishable body must put on imperishability" (v. 53 NRSV). I explained to Cheryl that because her physical body was no longer serving her, God was going to give her a new body—likening it to taking off an old coat and putting on a new garment, perfect and pain free.

The third scripture, I explained to Cheryl, was really for her children and husband so they could begin to visualize what heaven might be like through the words of Jesus in the Gospel of John 14:1-6a, 18-19, 27-28. I asked the family what they visualized as a perfect place for Cheryl. They all laughed and said that for sure there would need to be a Royals baseball team.

Before I read verses 18-19, I asked them if they believed in angels or that their mother would be with them in some way. Then I read, "I won't leave you as orphans. I will come to you. Soon the world will no longer see me, but you will see me. Because I live, you will live too." Then I quickly read the verses regarding "peace I leave with you; my peace I give to you." Of all the Gospel scriptures, I believe these are hugely important for a peaceful death.

The reading of Romans 8:38 as the final scripture helps reassure the family that "nothing can separate us from God's love in Christ Jesus our Lord." By reading this scripture, I encouraged Cheryl's family to go to places that she loved and speak often of her. I assured them that talking to her (even though they might not be able to see her) will help them remember any wise advice she might have given them before: "You will hear her in your heart and mind."

Lastly, I explained to the family that I was going to anoint Cheryl to ready her for her new birth. Because I was standing at the foot of the bed, I anointed her feet first and thanked God for all of the ways that Cheryl had used them to live fully and be wonderfully present whenever her family needed her. I next anointed her hands and thanked God for all of the ways she had cared for her family, citing all of the birthday cakes she had baked so lovingly. Lastly, I anointed her head with gratitude for her understanding and capacity to live fully in this world.

At that point, I invited everyone around the bedside to reach out to put a hand on Cheryl that we might share a prayer. Then I led them in a prayer that went something like this: "Oh Gracious, Eternal God, we are so grateful for Cheryl and all that she did to serve you, her family, and her community in this life. We ask that you be with her at this time and in your perfect time allow her to move into her new spiritual body. Bless her family with assurance of the gospel message of eternal life. We pray all this in the name of your son, Jesus the Christ who still teaches us to pray . . . [then pray the Lord's Prayer or recite the Twenty-Third Psalm]." If the person is still breathing, you might end the bedside service with a song.

Within a few minutes, Cheryl passed into eternity. We all stood vigil for a few minutes. At times like this, I try to gauge what the family will need. Do they want a few minutes alone with the deceased, or do they need to leave the room while you stay for a while? Trust that God will lead you in this minute to know what would be best for those present. In Cheryl's situation, the children and other family members started to leave the room within about five minutes. I left the room shortly thereafter, giving the husband a few minutes alone with her.

In this case study, the death occurred in the hospital, which means the medical people immediately took charge once we came out of the room. If the death occurs in the home, you may need to help the family with next steps of calling a funeral home or 911.

Once the person has passed, there may be questions about cremation or burial of the body. Again, this is a sensitive subject and you must consider the demographic of your church. More recently a large percentage of people have planned for cremation. Especially in situations where there may be financial needs, you might explain that cremation is usually less expensive. Theologically, I explain with the traditional text of "ashes to ashes and dust to dust" (Book of Common Prayer, OxfordReference .com). At this point, the family needs to know what to expect from you and the church. They are feeling powerless. Give the family your contact information and let them know when you will talk with them again. This allows them to know how you are going to walk with them through their loved one's death. Most people go through the death of a loved one only a few times in their lives, and it is important for you to be the church during these most sacred hours. Aftercare again is critical for the family and essential ministry of the CCMs.

After Death Has Occurred

If you arrive at the home, hospital, or hospice after the person has died:

o   Pray.

o   Be a calming presence.

o   The best response is to say first, "I'm so sorry."

o   Take time to assess the needs of the various people present in the room.

o   Invite hospital, hospice, or care staff to join the service. They certainly will have their moments of grief. They will feel the loss as surely as the family does, and this is a powerful ministry to them.

If the Body Is Present

o   Reading scripture similar to what was noted in Cheryl's story is appropriate.

o   Ask if you may anoint the body. The anointing of the body is not to be feared. It is biblical and extends a gracious holiness that both dispels fears and creates a holy service.

o   Pray with thanksgiving for the ways that this person served with their hands (anoint hands) or their feet (anoint feet).

Before Leaving

o   Wait until after the mortuary comes for the body to talk about next steps.

o   Make a plan with the responsible family or friends.

o   Provide your contact information to the family (business card, email, and phone numbers).

o   Collect their contact information.

o   Agree on a time when you or the pastor might be able to meet with the family to plan a service, if needed.

o   Always exit with a prayer and word of comfort.

Funeral Planning

Planning a funeral service is one of the most important elements of care that a pastor can ever do for a family. Although funeral planning is usually reserved for the pastor, there are many opportunities for CCMs to help care for the family. For example, volunteers can provide food, transportation, childcare, pet sitting, setting up a memorial table at the visitation, and so on.

In preparation for such a meeting, encourage the family to have everyone present who would want to help plan the service.

o   Take your Bible and hymnal.

o   Identify a family spokesperson.

o   Before entering the home, take a deep breath and pray to center yourself.

o   When you enter, introduce yourself and ask the names of everyone present and their relationship to the deceased.

o   At this moment they are waiting for you to lead. They are counting on you to take charge and help them go through this awkward, unknown "darkest valley." Express to the family that you are honored and humbled to be part of this sacred time with them.

o   Explain that you have three purposes in mind.

  – Honor their loved one.

  – Care for them.

  – Plan a service of worship and give thanks to God.

o   Once you have stated the purposes, invite them to pray.

If you are able to set up the meeting this way, the family will begin to relax and trust that you know how to lead them through this time. You might find it helpful to prepare a worksheet that helps you collect the information for the service. This includes but is not limited to the following:

o   Time and date

  – Will family be traveling?

  – Check the availability of the sanctuary, pastor, CCM or other key volunteer, or musician.

o   Funeral home, church, or other venue

o   Significant life events of the deceased

o   Significance of the deceased to others

o   Important adjectives that describe the person with stories that fit the descriptor

o   Faith story of the deceased

o   Requested scripture (be prepared with scriptures that you think might be appropriate)

o   Requested music (be prepared to offer music suggestions)

o   You might show them a funeral bulletin of a service that you have previously officiated.

o   Logistics

o   Important questions to ask about logistics include:

  –   When and where would the family like to have the service? Invite them to use your church, even if they are not members. This is a great evangelistic tool.

  –   Which mortuary did they choose?

  –   How many people might be expected at the service?

  –   Does anyone have special needs (such as persons who use wheelchairs, who are blind, or who are hard of hearing)?

  –   Do they also want a graveside service?

  –   Do family members want to speak at the graveside?

  –   Are there other special requests?

Many times a family would like to have two or three people other than the pastor speak. I state very early in the conversation my own experiences in this regard. I explain that I would be glad to take all their comments (written or spoken) and weave them into a eulogy. I tell them that I have found that having someone else try to speak can be a mistake. Many times people break down or say something that is not helpful. I remind them that people are vulnerable and mourning can take many forms.

I tell the family that the best time for an "open microphone" is at a gathering after the service. Sharing together in a more relaxed atmosphere can help the grieving process begin to move forward toward healing. Sharing can make for a wonderful time of celebration.

If the family insists on having other speakers:

o   Set a limit on how many can speak; a good rule of thumb is no more than two.

o   Agree on the amount of time each will speak, usually no more than three to five minutes each.

o   Tell them you would like to meet with the person(s) to avoid repetition of stories and to walk through the order of service to ensure all will go smoothly.

o   Tell the speakers to prepare no more than one page of material, single-spaced. This will take about five minutes to read.

In the Days before the Service

o   Plan to call and check on the family.

o   CCMs or volunteers can help with calls especially if they have been introduced into the circle or if they will be involved in after-care for the family. If the CCM has been on a long journey with the deceased and family, they may be asked to participate in the service if they feel comfortable doing so.

o   Design a service that has prayers, scriptures, music, and a sermon that will bless the family, celebrate the life of the deceased, and honor God.

o   Prepare to make a copy of your sermon available, if requested.

Bulletin

A good bulletin is a detail that assures the family and attendees that your church cares about the service, and by extension, that you care for them. This important detail will help you care for those in attendance. There will probably be people at the service who are unchurched. It is a good idea to print out the scripture readings and any liturgy in the bulletin. This allows people to take the bulletin home for further reflection.

o   A good bulletin also allows for extra details, such as directions to the cemetery or an invitation to a meal after the service.

o   You may include poems or have the obituary printed on the back of the bulletin.

Preparing the Sermon

As you prepare the sermon, be aware that you are crafting a life message that not only helps people celebrate and smile but also gives purpose and meaning to the life of the deceased person. You may want to set the person's picture in front of you as you write. This will remind you to do everything you can to honor the deceased and be helpful to the family. As you decide on stories remember the following:

o   Choose life lessons.

o   Use adjectives that will help people see the big picture.

o   Include the person's spiritual or faith story.

o   Pray and think through the script so that your words bring assurance and delve into the theological questions.

o   Help people connect the dots in a person's life.

o   Create an image of the place that God has created for the deceased person (John 14).

In the Event of a Sudden Death

o   Help the family remember that God weeps with them and that God, whose only Son died at an early age, surely knows their sorrow better than anyone (Romans 8).

o   If appropriate, remind them that accidents happen and that no one is to blame.

o   In the case of suicide, extend mercy and grace, knowing that everyone is hurting.

- Remind the family how mental illness problems or untreated depression can go undetected.

- Emphasize that no one is to blame.

- Drive home the point that God has great mercy on people who have made this choice, but that this is not the way any life should have to end.

- Quote a point in your doctrine for support.

When you have a congregation of unchurched teenagers and the deceased has died by either accident or suicide, you have an incredible opportunity to do what the church can do best: offer the assurance of eternal life and the opportunity to live life in ways that honor God and the deceased. As difficult as these situations might seem, be encouraged. These might be some of the most important times that you will have as a person of faith to make a difference. If you need help in preparing a message for a particular or difficult situation, seek out mentors who can help you or find texts that can offer guidance such as *Just in Time! Funeral Services* by Cynthia Danals (published by Abingdon Press).

Funeral Directors

Try to develop a relationship with the funeral home director who can tell you what is offered and the procedures. For example, the director will help you determine if you are to ride with the family to the graveside or drive your own car. The funeral director may have also collected an honorarium for your services from the family. Usually the mortuary will provide:

o casket or urn,

o plot or niche space,

o flowers,

o processional to the cemetery,

o visitation time, which can be at the mortuary or at the church,

o obituary in the local paper,

o   guest book, and

o   envelopes for donations.

The Day of the Service

o   Arrive early. CCMs can be especially helpful with setup.

o   Make sure the sanctuary is prepared for the family.

o   Have a volunteer, CCM, or another pastor present to help care for the family.

o   If you are conducting the service in an unfamiliar place, learn the layout of the chancel, family rooms, restrooms, and so on.

o   Pray before greeting the family.

o   Greet the family when they enter.

o   Lead the family to the location where they can store their belongings, and show them where the restrooms are located.

o   Allow them time to go into the sanctuary and observe the setup for the service.

Visitation before the Service

If the family is having a visitation before the service, prepare the family before guests start arriving. Understand this may be the first time they have experienced something like this.

o   Pray with the family. Offer a prayer of comfort and assurance for the healing that this time might offer.

o   Have the family center themselves in front of the casket.

o   Encourage them with the idea that everyone is coming to offer them love and support.

o   Make sure their needs are covered: provide bottles of water, tissues, and chairs.

o   Tell them the care team is there if they have any other need.

Before the Service Begins

o   Before the service, stand with the family to allow them one last time to view the body before the casket is closed.

o   Once the casket is closed, invite the family to gather in a comfortable space away from where the service will be conducted. This is a time to get them emotionally and mentally ready.

o   Your leadership in these preservice moments is crucial.

- Give them clear instructions about how you will lead them in and where to sit.

- Emphasize your intentions to celebrate the life of their loved one, to comfort them, and to worship God.

- When they see your readiness, they will feel as if they are in good hands and will find the courage to move forward.

- If you have conducted funerals before, you are familiar with what happens and what to expect, but it will be a completely new experience for many of the family members. Their grief may paralyze them in a number of ways. A well-planned funeral service should be between forty-five minutes to an hour long. Any longer and all of the unchurched people may assume that you preach that way all the time and will be glad they only come to funerals at your church. That is not what you want.

- In any event, you want to end on a high note! The deceased is with God today. "Let's hold on to each other and help the family as they live forward." Do not be hesitant in your hope! Radiate your faith so that even the unchurched will want to come back for more. It is hard to imagine a greater tool for growing your church than a well-thought-out funeral.

Redemption Story 10: A Young Pastor's Story

Recently, a young pastor called to ask about how to care for his community. The community had just suffered the death of a teenager one week, and then the next week, a four-year-old had been tragically killed.

We talked about being clear with the congregation. I suggested that perhaps he could prepare a two- or three-week sermon series based around the "Why" questions. Why did God let this happen? Why do bad things happen to good people? Why do we hurt so badly? What did we do to deserve this?

I encouraged him to engage volunteers to help him continue visiting the families. The pastor's presence was important, but he needed to mentor and guide others in this care process too. We talked about helping others know the right thing to say. Sometimes, not saying anything is best. Just your compassion and presence are all that are required.

I remembered a father whose fourteen-year-old had suffered from depression and had completed suicide. He said one particular friend didn't try to say anything but just hugged him and allowed him to cry. Sometimes less is better. Besides, no words can take away the pain.

I also encouraged this young pastor to offer a five- to six-week class on grief. Good grief curricula are available, such as *The Will of God* by Leslie Weatherhead (published by Abingdon Press), *When Bad Things Happen to Good People* by Rabbi Harold Kushner (published by Schocken Books) , or *Why?* by Adam Hamilton (published by Abingdon Press). These are classics that help us navigate life's most difficult questions.

Last, I suggested the pastor put on his calendar important dates to call or send a card. Birthdays and dates of death are especially important. Anniversaries are sure to stir up memories and feelings.

Follow-Up Care

Aftercare is so important! Plan how you will follow up and identify who will help you. Without a plan, the aftercare would fall between the cracks of everything else that happens in ministry.

o   Make phone calls on a specific timetable, from either the pastor or the CCM.

o   Note birthdays, dates of death, wedding anniversaries, and holidays. Schedule sending a note or making a call at these times. These can be from either the pastor or the CCM.

o   Invite the family to attend any services of remembrance, such as All Saints' Day.

o   Continue to call even years after the event. You will be a hero (not that you are seeking to be one, but you will find that the family is so glad that you still remember their loved ones).

o   Send grief books with notes every four months after the date of death. Include scripture in the notes and offer comfort and hope. Two very helpful grief books are *When the One You Love Is Gone* by Rebekkah Miles and *Beyond the Broken Heart* by Julie Yarbough (published by Abingdon Press). These texts can also be used for grief support groups. Invite family members to attend a grief support group. They may need multiple invitations to begin with a group or perhaps a trusted CCM could attend with them for their first meeting or two.

Additional Thoughts about Redemption

Remember that God has anointed you to do this holy work.

o   What you do offers redemption and restoration to individuals, families, your community, and truly to the whole world.

o God also anoints you to help others in your congregation to find their calling, their ways to minister and care for others.

o Caring for the congregation is not a solo task; it is a way of living together as the body of Christ.

Assessing Your Setting

o Do you currently have:

- A written bedside memorial?

- An approach for planning a funeral?

- A template or sample of a bulletin for a memorial service or funeral?

o Do you have key phrases that you incorporate into your funeral services?

o How do you articulate your personal theology about death and resurrection?

o How do you walk with a family when death is imminent?

- What is your standard to lead the family through the death process?

- Do you go immediately when the family calls?

- How do you personally feel about anointing a dead body?

o How do you care for the family after a loved one dies?

- What standard of care do you follow?

- What is your plan for follow-up care for the first and subsequent years?

o How do you articulate the gospel message of hope to people who are non- and nominally religious?

o   Is your funeral service prepared to:

   –   honor the deceased?

   –   comfort the family?

   –   invite people who are non- or nominally religious to receive the gospel message of resurrection and hope?

o   Can you cite an example of redemption happening in the midst of a family's journey through the dark valley of death?

   –   What events helped that redemption to happen?

Chapter Twelve

Documentation and Logistics

Notes for the Trainer

In chapter 3, we introduced the topic of documentation and logistics, and explained why we believe you must carefully plan for these aspects of your Congregational Care Ministry. We encouraged you to develop your own church's documentation and logistical flow. This chapter (chapter 12) takes the next step, and provides a framework for you to build on, equipping you to create the systems and tools you'll need in your own unique context. You will need to do some work on your own before you use this chapter for training your CCMs. You should develop a clearly defined documentation system and iron out the logistics before presenting this information to CCM trainees, so that they understand what to do and how to do it. Refer to chapter 3 for pointed questions to help you design the documentation system and logistical flow that will work best for your congregation.

Three General Steps

Begin this session by explaining the three general steps to providing excellent care through the Congregational Care Ministry model. Say: *In this model, there are three simple and general steps to provide care effectively as a congregation.*

o Intake and Dispatch—Director and Dispatcher curate and assign each care request to a CCM.

o Follow Up—CCMs receive their assignments weekly and follow up with the person requesting care.

o Documentation—After each assigned follow-up, CCMs document their interaction.

In this chapter we will discuss how to do each of these steps effectively and efficiently. Before we delve into each step, let's discuss the tools and technology that can be utilized as a team to accomplish our goals.

Introduce the tools and technology you have chosen to utilize. Explain the expectations surrounding usage, usernames and passwords, and so on. We have found it useful to show a quick tutorial explaining how to use the basic functions. Be ready and willing to answer questions and help individuals who may find the technology intimidating or difficult to navigate. If this is not your strength either, consider recruiting a tech-savvy volunteer to introduce these elements. Assure CCMs that paper documentation is an option for those who are intimidated by a digital format.

Intake and Dispatch

Say: *Now that we have the tools and technology, let's discuss how we utilize them within our three-step process. Our first step, Intake and Dispatch, includes collecting all prayer and care requests and assigning them to CCMs.*

Explain the process of how a congregant can request prayer or care at your church. Share how the requests are curated and documented, and then how and when CCMs receive their care assignments for the week.

Follow-Up

Say: *Once a CCM has received their assignments for the week, the next step is to follow up with those assignments.*

Explain the process for CCMs to follow up. What are the expectations surrounding follow-up timeliness and confidentiality? If there is confusion around a prayer request or who to contact, how will CCMs discern the next step? Perhaps a flow chart similar to the one in chapter 3 would be helpful. Remind participants of all previous training modules—encourage them to listen and follow all guidelines surrounding meeting in person and how to handle specific types of prayer and care requests. Remind them to pray with the one who requested prayer.

Documentation

Say: *After you complete each follow-up call or visit, you must document it. Remember the importance of confidentiality! Do not share any information exchanged in these confidential calls or visits with anyone outside of the Congregational Care Ministry. We do ask that you document details like date, type of call, and any important notes like upcoming special dates, and so on. If there are red flags or warning signs, please reach out to a pastor to determine how to proceed.*

Explain the documentation process for CCMs. All related paperwork, including referrals, family contact information, safety and self-care contracts, pastoral care worksheet, and history of care worksheets are included in *The Caring Congregation Ministry: Care Minister's Manual.* Share how information is stored and how to utilize the technology to document. Remind them why confidentiality is so important, while also maintaining that record keeping is equally important to capture an accurate picture of the care provided on behalf of the church.

CCM Expectations

As your basic training modules come to a close, be sure to articulate exact expectations for how many hours of care a CCM should be providing each week. Encourage your CCMs to remain open with you about scheduling conflicts and any accommodation needs they may need in order to provide quality care on behalf of the church.

1. Each CCM receives ____ people to call/visit per week/month.

2. Each CCM is responsible for following up and making sure the visits happen. If you cannot visit that month, ask for assistance from another CCM as a sub. Be sure to communicate that to the people you normally visit.

3. It is the role of the Dispatcher to communicate new assignments.

Redemption Story: A Grieving Young Woman's Story

I read a card from a young woman who had written that her grandfather had passed away recently. I put the card into the usual pile for sympathy and grief, knowing that it would be addressed. But something kept bringing to my mind the young woman who had written the card. By that afternoon, I could not stand it any longer and responded to the note with a phone call.

The call began as usual: "Hi, how are you? This is Pastor Karen calling." Before I could extend my sympathy, the young woman's voice broke and she said, "How did you know to call?" She went on to say she had just returned from the doctor, where she just learned that she had cancer.

That call hit me like a ton of bricks. What I came to understand was that God had been responding to me as I had been praying over the cards.

Lord God, we come to you with gratitude for your presence as we walk alongside people in crisis. We confess to you that we can be fearful or unsure as we approach traumatic situations so we ask that you help us to prayerfully follow your lead. Help us to be a conduit of your peace, hope, and redemption that surely your kingdom might come. All this we pray in Christ's name. Amen.

Part Three
Caring for People in Crisis

Chapter Thirteen

Crisis and Trauma

A s I (Karen) sat with my pastoral colleague, she told me how she had endured five miscarriages in the course of just a little more than a year. She helped me learn more about her grief and the silence she had kept as she continued to do her ministry. As I listened, it opened up my heart to a greater understanding of the depth of this trauma.

Such traumatic situations and learning "opportunities" are common to pastors and CCMs across the country. As challenging as these traumatic moments are across our communities, they offer an opening for the church to bring Christlike healing. This chapter will address some very current situations and how we might be equipped to lead people out of the darkest of moments.

Basic Understanding of Crisis and Trauma

Let us take a moment to differentiate between the words *crisis* and *trauma*. For our purposes in this text, the word *crisis* will help us name what the *acute situation* is such as miscarriage, sexual assault, or financial loss. *Trauma* will be the *long-term effects* of the crisis event and how the situation affects our physical, emotional, relational, and spiritual well-being.

Our depth of understanding of crisis and the resulting trauma is many times built out of our own life situations. Whenever I would be interviewing candidates for a particular ministry in the church, the most important question (in my mind) was to ask them what event in their lives helped them draw closer to God or the Christian community at such times. These questions always opened my eyes to their strengths and how they might fit best into our ministry.

One particular time I was interviewing different people to be my assistant. There were two very qualified candidates, but when I asked this question to the person who was awarded the job, she told me the story of how her four-year-old was run over in front of the family's house. At that point she was nearly six years out from the event and she was able to relay the event and how the church came to help the family over the weeks and years ahead. By her composure and capacity to tell her story, I knew this woman could walk alongside me when any crisis happened. Plus, I hope that our work together continued to offer her a depth of healing greater than she expected.

Some theologians speak of three different orders of suffering. The first order is where things cannot be controlled such as grief, illness, and separation/divorce. The second order is caused by acts of human evil such as murder, violence, prejudice, and war. Now in recent years the third order of suffering is described as a type of despair and hopelessness that grabs people in the midst of the first- or second-order suffering and keeps them stuck in their pain, unable to move forward. Such things as a mass shooting can impose such powerlessness and PTSD. As the church we must continue to infuse the world with the gospel message of resurrection and help people rise up in the midst of pain. What I believe to be true is this: *A crisis can crush, paralyze, anger, drive us to despair, or . . . it can propel us to greater visions of purpose and mission than we thought possible.*

A crisis provides us opportunity for great growth. Every experience is a teacher. Our greatest growth can happen when we embrace tough moments with gratitude and allow them to shape us into new creatures in Christ.

As the caregivers and sojourners who walk alongside people through crisis and trauma, it is so helpful to have a degree of experience of similar pain in our own lives. One great mentor of mine always emphasized to me the importance of true empathy as she said, "We must reveal to heal." I have passed along this sage advice to hundreds in their journey that they might have the courage to share their stories as they seek more complete healing.

That is why people who are wounded healers are many times the best caregivers as they understand more fully the long-term trauma that a person might face. Many times, people see hope through the lives of those who have lived through similar situations and not only survived but thrived in the aftermath.

Three Immediate Basics as You Respond to Any Crisis

1. Pray for guidance, strength, and assurance that you might hear God's voice. So many times, I have felt inadequate or fearful as I drive toward the situation. We absolutely must be grounded in God's grace and love as we walk into any situation.

2. Respond quickly. Once you know a crisis has occurred, respond immediately by calling your pastor (as a CCM) for direction or going to the scene yourself if you cannot reach the pastor. Do not be a lone ranger, but rather enlist others to help.

3. Be the presence of Christ. Our job is not to offer expertise in any logistical way (although there are exceptions) but rather to offer spiritual care that is needed during the critical moments. Sometimes you do not need to say a word but by merely being present you may be sharing the most important gift.

It is absolutely essential that our own theology as people of faith be well thought out. Probably most important, remember that crisis and trauma are not God's will for our lives but rather the result of living in an imperfect world where bad things happen. God is with us through the crisis and helps us have our own moments of resurrecting up out of the trauma. As caregivers, it is essential to be able to assure people that God is with them, helping them to make it through the pain and then to eventually help them rise up into new creatures in Christ.

What to say and do will become clearer as we go through a few different types of crisis noted in this chapter. More situations are noted in the participant workbook including anger, abuse, job search/financial care, grief, infidelity, and utilizing case studies for these. Taking time to visit with other CCMs and pastors about the different situations listed will help you feel more confident when you are given the "opportunity" to care.

Cancer and/or Chronic Illness

Talking Points/Information

- o Love the physical part of you that carries the cancer or other chronic illness.

- o Thoughtfully take care of your body through diet, exercise, and rest.

- o Focus on treatment opportunities.

- o Find joy within adversity when possible.

- o Ask supporters to be with you where you are—whether in pain or as cheerleaders.

Scriptures

- o Psalm 121

- o Psalm 63:8

- o Isaiah 43:1-7

- o Lamentations 3:32

- o 2 Corinthians 4:8

o   Philippians 4:13

o   Hebrews 12:2

o   James 5:13-15

o   1 Peter 5:7

Prayer

Lord, you said that when we walk through the water, you will be with us; we are precious in your sight and you love me. In this time of health trial and adversity, I need to be aware of your presence more than ever. Lord, some days I feel hard-pressed on every side, but with you near I do not feel crushed. I am struck down at times, but not destroyed. When this disease makes me feel as if I don't have any control, Lord, give me strength and courage, hold me in the palm of your hand, and give me peace. Amen.

Suggested Reading and Resources

o   *Jesus Calling* by Sarah Young

o   *Jesus Lives* by Sarah Young

o   *The Will of God* by Leslie Weatherhead

o   *What about Divine Healing?* by Susan Sonnenday Vogel

o   Cancer support groups

o   Ongoing pastoral care and counseling opportunities from the church

o   The American Cancer Society

o   Caring Conversations (www.practicalbioethics.org)

Divorce

Talking Points/Information

o   Your worth is not tied to your marital status. At your creation, God called you "very good."

o Divorce is a painful split.

o Dating immediately after a divorce can stifle the healing you need, because you might try to find your healing in another person.

o You will need to eventually forgive, for your own sake. Forgiveness blesses you as you release the control your ex-spouse had over your feelings.

o Forgiving too soon can be hazardous to your healing. When you do forgive, you may decide to do it with your own ritual (for example, writing the word forgiveness on paper and burning it).

o Saying "I forgive you" to an ex-spouse often incites more anger and pain.

o If you are a parent, do not treat your kids, regardless of their ages, as your caregivers or best buddies.

o Make space for your kids (of all ages) to share their pain even if their pain causes you guilt or hurt. They need you.

o Teenage children need particular attention during divorce: they are more likely to behave in overly sexualized ways, adopt an eating disorder, or cut themselves.

Scriptures

o Genesis 1:31

o Luke 13:10-17

o John 8:1-11

o Romans 8:1

o Philippians 3:12-15

o 1 John 4:7-20

o Revelation 21:5

Prayer

God of infinite love and understanding, pour out your healing spirit upon me as I make a new beginning. Where there is hurt or bitterness, grant healing of memories and the ability to put behind me the things that are past. Where feelings of despair or worthlessness flood in, please nurture a spirit of hope. Give me confidence that by your grace tomorrow can be better than yesterday. Heal my children and help me minister to them. I pray for other family and friends in Jesus Christ my Savior. Amen.

Suggested Reading and Resources

o *Radical Recovery: Transferring the Despair of Your Divorce into an Unexpected Good* by Suzy Brown

o Divorce recovery groups for men, women, and children

o Marriage and family therapists

Infertility, Miscarriage, and Stillbirth

Talking Points/Information Regarding Infertility

o Today one in six couples (17 percent) is infertile.

o Infertile women have depression scores that are basically indistinguishable from those of women with cancer, heart disease, or hypertension. The psychological toll of infertility cannot be underestimated.

o Infertility is the inability to conceive after trying for twelve months.

o Primary infertility is not being able to have a live birth of your first child. Secondary infertility is inability to have a live birth of a child after previously having a child.

o Listen and allow the woman/couple time to share their feelings of pain.

o Connecting them with others who have had this experience is helpful.

Suggested Reading

o *Hannah's Hope: Seeking God's Heart in the Midst of Infertility, Miscarriage, and Adoption Loss* by Jennifer Saake

o *When Empty Arms Become a Heavy Burden: Encouragement for Couples Facing Infertility* by Sandra Glahn and William Cutter

o *The Infertility Companion: Hope and Help for Couples Facing Infertility* by Sandra Glahn and William Cutter

o *Empty Womb, Aching Heart: Hope and Help for Those Struggling with Infertility* by Marlo Schlaesky

o *Grace Like Scarlett: Grieving with Hope after Miscarriage and Loss* by Adriel Booker

Talking Points/Information Particular to Miscarriage

o Miscarriage is losing a fetus before it is able to survive independently, usually any time prior to twenty-eight weeks.

o Recognize that mothers and fathers may feel very similar pain and expressions of grief, but they may also have very different and what may seem like extreme emotions.

o Many times people grieve silently, remembering their miscarriage dates without saying a word to anyone. The due date may be a trigger for grief.

o A miscarriage will cause physical and hormonal changes that need to be respected.

Scriptures

o Romans 8:24-25—Hope for what we do not yet have.

o Isaiah 40:31—Hope in the Lord will renew your strength.

o   Matthew 5:4 (NRSV)—"Blessed are those who mourn, for they will be comforted."

o   1 Peter 5:7—Cast your care upon God that you may be restored by grace.

o   Romans 12:12—Be patient and faithful.

o   Jeremiah 29:11—God has a plan and a future for you.

o   Philippians 4:6-7—Present your requests to God that you might have peace.

o   2 Corinthians 1:3-4—God consoles us in our affliction.

Prayer

Lifegiving God, we come to you hurt and broken, trying to understand why this life that we had hoped to bring into this world is now gone from us. We only know that where there was sweet expectation, now there is bitter disappointment; where there was hope and excitement, there is a sense of failure and loss. We have seen how fragile life is and nothing can replace this life, this child, whom we have loved before seeing, before feeling it stirring in the woman. In our pain and confusion we look to you, Lord God, in whom no life is without meaning. Prepare my body and please bring to us the right doctors and modern miracles that we might create a child. Give us your compassion that we might live forward. In Christ's name. Amen.

Personal Story and Suggestions from Rev. Joy Dister-Dominguez

Recently I came across a journal I used as a teenager outlining my dreams and goals. While most have changed, one has not: to have children. Two and a half years ago when my partner and I first began to struggle with unexplained infertility, I went through a process of grief, sadness, and shame. "Why me, God? Why us?" When our journey brought us to IVF after prayerful consideration I thought, "This will solve our problems." Our first egg retrieval went well, although painfully, and soon after, we transferred the perfect embryo, and waited. At our six-week appointment we saw a strong heartbeat and were told we'd have less than a 5 percent chance of miscarriage. We were so happy; I cherished every moment, even though I had horrible morning sickness. I began to dream of our future with our baby.

We entered our nine-week appointment, excited to see how our baby had grown. The next day we had plans to tell our parents; our hearts were bursting with joy. But I knew something was wrong when we didn't see our baby right away on the sonogram. The look on the doctor's face said it all: the baby vanished, gone. Shock, disbelief, anger, and grief took my breath away. The doctor and nurse left the room; I hugged my partner tight as I cried and wailed, and he cried with me in disbelief. The following days I had a D&C (dilation and curettage, a procedure to remove tissue), and I was numb with excruciating grief. I felt so much despair and hollowed out; our dreams of this little boy and our family were gone. Our parents grieved with us, a loss of a grandson and their dreams too. Yet, I knew that Jesus wept with us. I leaned on God to make it through each day, some days just to get out of bed. Years later, I still have my moments of deep despair.

Months later we tried again, and months after that, again. Another round of IVF, more tries, other early miscarriages, and the grief continued to build. Someone said to me, "I don't know how you do it." I replied, "I have no other choice. I feel called to be a mother. We feel called to be parents." I am preparing my body for the third round of IVF with the hope and prayer that this time will be different, and someday we'll hold our baby. I've found safe, supportive friends to process this compounded grief, and I am intentional in self-care, especially on difficult days where I deeply grieve our babies who are with God.

Information and Suggestions from Rev. Joy

- There can be a great deal of shame surrounding infertility, miscarriage, and stillbirth.

- It is your job as a pastor or CCM to have a basic understanding of these situations and respond accordingly. Create a safe environment for women or partners to talk without shame, judgment, and insensitive comments. It is important to honor the feelings people have while not trying to project assurances of the future. "Oh, just relax, it will happen" is painful to hear, rather than comforting.

- Pastors and CCMs should recommend women and partners to seek professional counseling, preferably from a psychologist who specializes in women's mental health, or spiritual direction. When appropriate, suggest a physical burial with a token or perform a short service of remembrance.

Miscarriage and stillbirths leave gaping holes emotionally and physically. The baby who was prayed for, and plans that were made get ripped away. Often family and friends do not know how to respond. Pastors and CCMs can respond with the ministry of presence: call and offer to show up with food, flowers, or gifts of remembrance. Do not offer cheap platitudes or try to make sense of the loss spiritually. A gentle reminder that God is present in their suffering, grieves with the loss of this baby, and is home their baby can help. Honor their feelings that will linger for days, months, and years. Remember sensitive dates such as Mother's Day and Father's Day, due dates, and loss dates, and help to honor the loss in special ways.

Rape/Sexual Assault

Talking Point/Information

o   It is not your fault.

o   You are made in the image of God.

o   You are not alone.

Scriptures

o   Psalm 23—God is with you in the midst of the valley.

o   Isaiah 43:1-5—Do not fear for I have redeemed you.

o   Psalm 57:1—I take refuge in the shadow of your wings until the storms pass by.

o   Psalm 71:20-21—You will revive and comfort me once again.

o   Psalm 126:5-6—May those who sow in tears reap with shouts of joy.

o   Psalm 143—Prayer for deliverance.

o   Psalm 147:3—God heals the brokenhearted and binds up their wounds.

o   John 4:4-24—God knows our stories and loves us beyond measure.

o   Matthew 11:28-30—Jesus will give rest to the weary.

o   Luke 13:10-17—The bent-over woman's story as Jesus calls her out of the corner to speak.

o   John 8:1-11—Be careful in interpreting the scripture that you do not believe what she is enduring is a sin but rather underline that God is with her, defending her.

o   Romans 8—Nothing can separate us from the love of God.

o   1 John 4—God is love and not about punishment.

Prayer

Lord, give me the grace to be honest—honest about my pain, honest about my feelings, honest about my anger, and honest about my questions. How could this have happened to me, God? Please lead me to trusted friends, mentors, and professionals who can help me process what has happened. Gracious God, help me be ever aware of your presence and remind me that I am a beloved child of God. In due time, Lord, help me rise up out of the ashes of this that I might help others regain their confidence and assurance that they are worthy. All this in Christ's name. Amen.

Suggested Reading

o   *Little Girl Lost: One Woman's Journey beyond Rape* by Leisha Joseph

o   *Survivor Care: What Religious Professionals Need to Know about Healing Trauma* by Christy Gunter Sim

Resources

o   Metropolitan Organization to Counter Sexual Assault (MOCSA), www.mocsa.org; in Kansas City, 913-642-0233 or 816-531-0233

Domestic violence, emotional abuse, sexual manipulation, and assault are important areas for pastors and CCMs to consider as possible care scenarios. Healing from this kind of trauma takes years, and in many cases can shape a person's life to either take on strength and purpose or it can cripple or paralyze the victim.

It has been my personal experience that spiritual care is critical to a greater sense of healing. It is critical for the church to partner with mental health practitioners, local police, and medical caregivers who would be able to be part of the healing team.

That being said, there is a high likelihood that violence and abuse will continue without being reported. Many victims may find themselves shamed or locked into a relationship that they do not feel free to report. It is important to note that many do not even understand that they are being preyed upon. The #MeToo movement has given victims a greater understanding of how prevalent this is and how to find their voice.

To heal you must reveal. Yet again, most victims can find themselves in situations where people will either blame them or say words like *consensual*, which will shut down their voices again.

There are so many great textbooks that can help you with facts and understanding in this regard. For our purposes, here is a condensed version of important points to consider as a spiritual guide:

o *Make sure your theological understandings ensure grace and strength.* When I, (Karen) finally revealed what was happening to me and the hell that my husband and I were living through, the first spiritual woman that I turned to offered me grace that felt like the balm of Gilead. She would listen deeply then offer me scriptures, daily devotional resources, a journal to write my prayers, and opportunities to bond with strong women of faith. Never before had I felt the arms of the church more fully or understood the gospel message of salvation more clearly.

o Because most victims feel depressed, unworthy, and ashamed, there is a need for counseling and medical assistance. For me, my weight fell down to eighty-seven pounds and I found myself compensating my pain by overworking and shutting some people out of my life. Be alert to symptoms that may need the help of other professionals.

o   If you hear of a predator or domestic violence situation going on, how do you proceed? This question varies with every situation. The most important thing to remember is to offer support to the victim. Most people in these situations feel that they have lost their agency and capacity to make good decisions. If they need to leave the situation, offer them prayers of encouragement and if needed help them find safe places to go. If it is a situation that means daily contact with their abusers, help them visualize themselves taking control and staying clear of any vulnerable situations with the abuser. If you feel like they may be in highly dangerous situations, help them develop plans and perhaps seek protection orders from the local police. Also, many of us as pastors and CCMs are court-mandated reporters. Check with your state laws to understand what you are required by law to do.

In all of these situations, listen for God's voice as the spirit will speak to us. As a pastor or CCM, find a trusted counselor, pastor, or colleague to help you think through how you can best respond. These are not situations for "lone rangers." Your care receiver will be eternally grateful if the situation is handled with great grace.

Gracious Loving God, thank you for your watchful, loving Spirit. Please use us to bring peace that passes understanding through our ministries. All this to honor the Wonderful Counselor, Prince of Peace. Amen.

Chapter Fourteen

Mental Health Ministry

*"Whenever the spirit from God came on Saul, David would take
up his lyre and play. Then relief would come to Saul;
he would feel better, and the evil spirit would leave him."*

—1 Samuel 16:23 NIV

The scriptures make it clear to us that the biblical characters suffered with depression and anxiety. And although they called them "[evil] spirits . . . from God," it is clear they were trying to find ways to relieve their suffering. Other scriptures include the laments of the psalmist along with the despair and depression of Job, Hagar, Naomi, and Judas. Sleepless anxiety is noted as Jacob in the scriptures wrestled with God night and day (one example from Genesis 32:22-32).

As we seek to do our part to help struggling people with their mental health, the faith community can be key to eliminating the stigmas and misunderstandings wrapped around mental health. We must help our congregations understand that this is not brought on by God or by evil spirits nor is it a character flaw or spiritual weakness. Rather it is a disease process. If we get a physical wound or injury we are quick to go to an urgent care. That same kind of urgency to seek professional help must be encouraged when people need a counselor, psychiatrist, or both. Breaking the stigma can best be done through classes, sermons, and one-on-one care where shame and denial are identified.

What We Know about Mental Illness

o   In almost all cases, mental illness is a function of chemical imbalance plus genetic predisposition combined with environmental factors.

o   MRI studies increasingly demonstrate that mental illness is best accounted for as differences in neurological functioning.

o   One in five American adults experience a mental illness in a given year.

o   Major mental illness reduced life expectancy by up to thirty years.

o   Sixty percent of people with mental illness do not receive treatment, usually because of stigma.

During the years of the Great Recession, suicide in the rural area where I (Karen) was raised was at a peak because of the unspoken shame and fear. The mental health struggles were many times dealt with by the guns or ropes in the closets of the farm or ranch families.

Even recently with a world pandemic, there are cases of suicide born out of despair, exhaustion, and PTSD.

As pastors and CCMs, we want to be of help with these situations. We may not be able to offer a full menu of mental health classes, but any size church can begin with creating connections with the mental health caregivers in your region who can brainstorm with you about how best to encourage care. No matter where you live, it can be challenging to find resources where you do not need to wait a week or more. That being said, it is essential for a church to create a list of resources ready to hand to congregants that will give them a starting point. This list of resources identifies trusted counseling and mental health services, local Alcoholics Anonymous/Narcotics Anonymous, safe shelters for abuse victims, national mental health hotlines, and food pantries, just to name a few.

As faithful CCMs and pastors offering spiritual guidance, our role is important. We offer hope and encouragement through scriptures and prayer that God is with the suffering and loves them during this challenging time. Again, we should be making sure that our theology reflects grace without judgment.

Key Scriptures to Consider

o   Psalms 27; 31; 69; 71; 91; 138; 139; 143

o   Lamentations 3:21-24

o   Matthew 11:28-30

o   John 14:27

o   Philippians 3:13-15; 4:4-7, 13

Ways to Address the Stigma Regarding Mental Health

o   Talk about mental illness, whenever you can and wherever you can.

o   Regularly host groups, panels, and classes focused on mental health.

o   Avoid using shaming words, such as crazy, psycho, insane, and so on.

o   Don't discriminate on the basis of mental illness for volunteer roles.

o   Talk about the value of counseling and medicinal interventions.

o   Collaborate with area clinicians on programming.

o   Give staff and volunteers access to "mental health first aid" training.

o   Find a mental health professional who can review your church's worship experience.

o   Take away guesswork by making as much of your ministry accessible online as possible.

As Pastors and CCMs, It Is Helpful to Know the Differences among the Mental Health Clinicians

o *Psychiatrists* are medical doctors specializing in mental illness. In most contexts these providers focus on medicinal interventions.

o *Psychologists* are doctoral-level clinicians using primarily traditional talk therapy to treat clients. They may also administer advanced testing (ADHD, IQ, personality, etc.).

o *Counselors/Therapists* are masters-level clinicians who usually use traditional talk therapy to treat clients. They may also offer tools like EMDR, neurofeedback, TMS, and hypnotherapy.

o *Substance Abuse Counselors* are, in many states, able to obtain licensure without an advanced degree, though most states require a licensure exam. They use talk therapy and support to assist those in recovery.

When helping a congregant choose a "Christian" counselor it is important to be aware of their theology, training methods, and values. Trained, trusted counselors should respect the diversity of clients, the goals of the client, and avoid imposing their own values, attitudes, and beliefs. All that being said, it is extremely important for you as a pastor or CCM to know the counselor has been vetted and know the person's values align with your congregation. Try to eliminate barriers that would prevent people from getting counseling such as:

o cost,

o location, and

o too many/too few options.

Prayer and meditation can be a hugely helpful tool for the struggling person. Daily meditation has been scientifically proven to increase the capacity of the brain to process at higher levels of reasoning. As you begin to care for someone, create a space of grace where they can feel accepted and heard. When they are ready, offer such meditation tools as the "Breath Prayer" that is noted in chapter 7. Another excellent method of praying is through journaling. Encourage them to acknowledge their pain followed by an acceptance of God's love and light readily available to them. Breathing deep and releasing their pain eases physiological stress. The importance of daily prayer rituals cannot be overstated. As a pastor or CCM our task is to model, encourage, and provide tools to develop these disciplines of prayer.

As you sit and care for those who are struggling mentally, the pastor or CCM must be clear (yet compassionate) about their own boundaries. For instance, be definite about when, where, and how long you will meet with this person. Do not overcommit or give your personal communication information too quickly. Be cautious and wise about the use of touch: it can be healing and comforting or confusing, hurtful, and unwelcome. All of these basic guidelines model for the person how to set their own healthy boundaries.

One great resource that you might have on your shelf is a book titled *The Depression Cure: The Six-Step Program to Beat Depression without Drugs* by Stephen Ilardi, PhD (Da Capo Press). This text is a great one to offer a class for your community. It highlights Therapeutic Lifestyle Changes (TLC) that include diet, exercise, light (sunshine or otherwise), socialization, sleep, and finding healthy activities to counter rumination patterns.

Even as we teach the TLC method and offer encouragement through spiritual methods, we must always be aware that a care plan for mental health should include mental health professionals. The church is most effective in mental health ministry when we promote the fullness of care.

Anxiety

Anxiety has been found to be as dangerous as depression. Thus it is important to be aware of a few of the symptoms:

o   Excessive worrying

o   Panic, fear, and restlessness

o   Sleep problems

o   Not being able to stay calm or still

o   Cold, sweaty, numb, or tingling hands or feet

o   Shortness of breath

o   Heart palpitations

o   Dry mouth

o   Nausea

If you note these symptoms, do not assume that you can help a person without more professional help. Address the possibility of seeking more help with the person. Also, remember these points:

o   Anxiety can be contagious and can hijack your ability to provide good care. Manage your own anxiety by taking a deep breath and controlling your tone of speech, pace, response, and follow-up questions or comments.

o   Stop to pray. This can break the cycle of anger, self-pity, or indecision that may be getting in the way of progress. Remember, you cannot control the other person's response or the outcome.

o   You are in control of the session's length. Generally, at the onset, tell the person you are meeting with that you have set aside a certain amount of time, perhaps an hour. The greater clarity you can give, the better it usually is. Setting boundaries in space (a quiet, safe place) and time (decided ahead of time) gives people a sense of structure and will help them manage their own anxiety better.

o   Allow yourself grace when dealing with complex or emotionally challenging situations. Remember, when we get down in the dirt with people as Jesus did with the woman in John 8, we can find ourselves in difficult circumstances. Do not be discouraged. Find a pastor, colleague, supervisor, or counselor to help you process your feelings.

Offer Comfort

The scriptures tell us, "Comfort, comfort my people!" (Isaiah 40:1). Always offer a next step for those who come to see you, even if it is just seeing them in worship next week.

Offer weekly check-ins with good boundaries. Who else on your team would offer helpful compassionate support? Are there courses that would help them find healthy socialization or greater understanding of their situation? Are there ways that they can serve others to find a renewed sense of purpose?

They have come to you, spilled their story, and offered you a part of their life that perhaps no one else has ever heard. You are acting on behalf of Christ and the church. What would Christ do for this lamb?

Helpful scriptures include:

o   Proverbs 12:25

o   Psalm 46:10

o   Psalm 91

o   Isaiah 43:1-5

o   1 Peter 5:7

One prayer tool you can share is a simple *ABC Prayer*

o   "A" is *acknowledge* how you are feeling, without judgment.

o   "B" is being aware of your *breath*. Breathing in peace, exhale your pain.

o   "C" is *choosing* to be full of love, light, grace, peace, and joy.

Suicide

The statistics are clear: suicide is on the rise in the United States, especially among some demographics. According to the National Institute of Mental Health, the suicide rate increased 31 percent from 2001 to 2017.

Increased rates of suicide are especially seen in younger people but also in older males (Statistics from the National Institute of Mental Health, January 2021) .

As church care providers we must understand our roles to address suicidality:

o   Develop a relationship with crisis resources in your community such as mental health centers, the local police, EMT services, fire department, and emergency rooms.

o   Remember you are not equipped to be a police officer, an EMT, or an emergency room physician.

o   Don't let the threat of suicide be a reason for violating boundaries.

   –   Case study: You receive a call at midnight from a person who is suicidal. What should a CCM do?

o   Develop guidelines your staff and volunteers can use and train them in their use, for example, knowing when to call 911.

o   Avoid the use of euphemisms and be direct and clear if you suspect someone might be suicidal. If you suspect someone is disingenuous in their threat, it is crucial to remain direct and follow the protocol. This communicates that you are taking their words seriously.

o   Don't leave a suicidal person alone until you are sure they are safe.

o   Make it OK to talk about. Ask every time if necessary if they have a plan or any intention of ending their life.

It is essential that we are alert for suicidal warning signs:

o   Talk about wanting to die or kill oneself

o   Looking for a way to kill oneself, such as searching online or buying a gun

o   Talk about feeling hopeless or having no reason to live

o   Talk about being a burden to others

o Sudden unexplained recovery of depressive symptoms or a sudden positive outlook

o Sleeping too little or too much

o Withdrawal or feeling isolated

o Displaying extreme mood swings

o Acting anxious or agitated, behaving recklessly

Responding to a Suicide

How do we immediately respond as Christian caregivers when a suicide happens? When a suicide happens, Jesus (in the form of you) must show up and the quicker, the better. Pray yourself up:

Gracious, loving God, this feels like the worst situation for this family and I know you have called me to be with them. Though I may feel fearful and inadequate, please bring to me a sense of peace, compassion, and strength that I can help the family through these moments. Help me to listen to your spirit as I search for the right words. Let the peace of Christ be with us as we move through this day. All this in the name of our healer, Jesus the Christ. Amen.

If possible, take along another pastor or CCM. In the situation of suicide there is likely to be many people who will need one-on-one care. This is not the time to be a lone ranger! Once you arrive, there may be people who are clustered in groups and others who need their space. Be cognizant of the people around you; even first responders may need you to offer a prayer for them.

We remember that for Jesus, getting down in the dirt was his way of helping people live through the crisis. With a suicide that may mean lying down on the floor with people or getting on your knees beside them. I remember when Joe took his life, I arrived at the house very shortly after the death and found Christine literally crying prostrate on the floor. At that point, I, along with other caregivers, got down on the floor with her. As if by osmosis, she eventually found the strength to sit up on the floor and then onto the sofa.

Other times when people are in a chair, I have knelt down beside them. Most every time, I have allowed them to cry on my shoulder or through an embrace. Again, allow God to lead you that you might do what is needed as you observe good, honoring boundaries while addressing the crisis of the moment.

It is normal for a family to test their theology with questions such as, "Why would God allow this? Where was God when Joe needed him?" It is at that point that the caregiver must respond clearly, yet tenderly. My standard answer for this question is that God was with Joe in the moment trying to get through to him, but because Joe's mind was not clear, even God could not get through.

Another common question is, "Do you think he (or she) is in hell?" This has long been a theological question that is still debated today depending on your beliefs. The United Methodist belief on suicide reads:

> We believe that suicide is not the way a human life should end. Often suicide is the result of untreated depression, or untreated pain and suffering. The Church has an obligation to see that all persons have access to needed pastoral and medical care and therapy in those circumstances that lead to loss of self-worth, suicidal despair, and/or the desire to seek physician-assisted suicide. We encourage the Church to provide education to address the biblical, theological, social, and ethical issues related to death and dying, including suicide. . . . A Christian perspective on suicide begins with an affirmation of faith that nothing, including suicide, separates us from the love of God (Romans 8:38-39). Therefore, we deplore the condemnation of people who complete suicide, and we consider unjust the stigma that so often falls on surviving family and friends.[1]

Of course, the big question of "why" did this happen will continue to be asked maybe even for months or years after the event. There will be lots of derivatives of this question:

o   Why didn't he/she talk to me?

o   Why did he/she do this to the family?

o   Why didn't I see this coming?

It is so important to allow enough time for people to process this event with you and others so they will hopefully find some peace in their souls. It is important for you to assure them that this is no one's fault. For Christine, Joe's mind was not clear, she had done all that she could, and it was not her fault. In the moment of crisis be clear that bad things happen to good people. A space of grace is essential—with no judgement . . . only grace.

From the very beginning it is important to use language that will not cause more harm. For instance, I never use the phrase "committed suicide" because theologically we "commit" sin and we certainly do not want the family to believe that the person has committed a sin (some may say murder). Rather say, "took his life," "completed" suicide, or "suicided." My personal choice is "completed suicide" because it helps people see that there is an important choice of language that I am making and many times they will ask why I say "completed" instead of "committed." This question offers a great opportunity for a theological conversation.

In those early moments of crisis, whoever has found the body may need extra care. This experience can cause long-term trauma. For you to be able to help the person learn to pray and release this memory is critical. Scripture can be helpful. Some helpful examples include 1 Corinthians 15:44, 49-57 and 2 Corinthians 4:-12, 17-18; 5:1-3. These scriptures can help us reframe to a place of hope as we remember that there is a spiritual body for us. As a caregiver, you may also have seen the body (and perhaps anointed the body) and you may need to seek your own prayer partner and counselor to help you process what you have seen.

Singing a familiar song can be helpful to calm the intensity of the situation. For Christine, we sang "Great is Thy Faithfulness." She said the following day she chose a different song. Music can be a powerful source of strength and peace in the midst of great pain, shock, and fear.

Like any drastic crisis, the complexity of suicide requires a team effort. To have CCMs who are checking in on the family is so important. The day Joe died, we immediately called in two CCMs who remained faithful caregivers for Christine.

If a multitude of people come to the house, it is good at some point to call everyone into a circle to help them reclaim their faith and be assured that the person is with God.

Very often families go through a moment when they feel shame about the event. As the spiritual leader, it is important that you help them understand it is not their fault and help them process the importance of speaking the truth about the situation. Those who have tried to hide the truth tend to take on a cloak of shame that disallows them from helping others and releasing their own pain.

One family who lost their daughter to suicide immediately went to that place of hiding the truth, but when we began to talk about how sharing the truth might help others, they began to change their mind. Their daughter had been sexually assaulted as a sophomore in high school and she did not tell anyone until she began to experience severe depression. She eventually completed suicide her freshman year in college. What the family found was that they were able to encourage people who had been sexually assaulted and those who might be fighting depression. Again, sit with people during these moments so you can help them walk through their emotions.

Besides pastoral care, long-term professional counseling is essential for the family of those who have completed suicide. As a pastor or CCM, encourage the person to seek out a counselor. You may also want a counselor to come to a grief group so the victims can begin to feel safe and familiar with the counselor. A special grief group for suicide victims can offer immeasurable help.

Key Strategies for Such a Specific Grief Group

Some specific strategies to keep in mind include:

o   Finding the right facilitator for such a group is key. That person must have a well-thought-out theology. Although not essential, some leaders who have lived through such an event can embody hope to the participants.

o   Encourage the participants to talk about their feelings and fears.

o   Help them to understand the church's stance on suicide.

o   Provide scriptures that will help them remember biblical characters who struggled with depression or anxiety, with some of them completing suicide. Such people as Naomi, Hagar, Moses, Samson, Job, Jonah, and Judas will provide them great examples.

o   When people are able to concentrate, provide books and curriculum that will give them words for what they are feeling. A skilled group facilitator can offer a thoughtful outline about a chapter of a book or an article that will help spark good conversation. That being said, the group discussion may need to go in another direction.

o   Be alert for those in the group who may not have spoken. Gently invite them to express their thoughts and make sure that you speak with them before they leave the group.

o   Other details to provide are tissues, name tags, and names of community resources such as mental health facilities. Remembering birthdays, date of death, and important holidays is an important way for the group to offer support to one another.

Assessing Your Community

1.   What are the primary mental health issues in your community?

2.   Who is most at risk?

3.   What community collaboration needs to happen?

4.   What steps do you need to take to establish a group to address a mental health issue?

Chapter Fifteen

Recovery Ministry

Never before in the history of humankind have we faced such a drastic need for recovery care. As of August 2019, *USA Today* reported that twenty-one million Americans struggle with substance addictions and that only one in ten of those addicted will receive treatment. The U.S. Surgeon General said that one in seven Americans will face substance abuse addiction. No doubt, every one of us can prayerfully say a name of someone close to us who is struggling.

> *Gracious healing God, we remember our family and friends who are in recovery or need to be. Thank you for your presence with them. Please help us to be there for them and to provide encouragement. All this in our Savior's name. Amen.*

Much of what we will be encouraging you to consider regarding recovery we have learned from CCMs and pastors who have dedicated much of their ministry to recovery because they have walked the walk. Like most churches that start a recovery ministry, Resurrection had an AA group that met twice a week down the far hall right beside a door to the outside so they could come and go without people seeing them. Just by this very action of room assignment we were perpetuating their shame. Most addicts do not want anything to do with the religious community because of the shame and secrets they are carrying. They associate judgment with the church instead of grace. So how do we create a recovery ministry where people can experience the true power of grace? First and foremost, like other ministries we need champions who understand from their own lives what it means to have a church family and a savior in their journey of recovery.

Pastor Tom Langhofer came to me early in his recovery. At that point he was a layperson who wanted to get involved with our care ministries. I asked him to observe and engage with our new, fledgling recovery ministry. For seven years, Tom came and helped as he could with the ministry. It became his passion. As Tom lived into his own recovery I encouraged him to take the CCM training. Then as the years went by I encouraged him to become a pastor. Tom gave up a very lucrative career in real estate to become a full-time recovery pastor. He is just one of many CCMs who eventually became pastors.

Essential Guidelines
for a Recovery Ministry

o   Find the right people who will draw others into the ministry: people who are willing to be vulnerable and tell their story to others. This may take time and several asks before they are willing to go public with their stories. Once they have an example like Tom, who they see is working on his recovery every day in the church, they are more likely to take the first step.

o   Partner more visibly with your community AA and NA groups. Ask them how you can help them build their programs.

o   If you are in a large town or city create a community advisory group that meets quarterly to brainstorm about how to tackle the addiction problems of your community. Branch out and invite other groups to be part of your recovery efforts. Invite local counselors, high school administrators, local police, rehab clinicians, hospitals, or any other local entity that seeks to give support to the individuals and families seeking recovery. Linking arms with others in your community gives your program credibility and greater visibility.

o   Create a Recovery Night if you are able. Provide a meal where participants can fellowship and connect. One of the key factors for addicts can be a sense of loneliness. They think they are the only ones who are living in this hell. When they share a meal with others and begin to share their journeys, barriers begin to break down. A sense of belonging to a group that accepts them is such a gift!

o   Instead of having a sermon or worship service at your recovery meetings, consider having one person give a meaningful witness or have a panel discussion where multiple people are sharing their stories.

o   Search out or create your own recovery ministry curriculum. The Life Recovery Program is one option.

o   Small group work is essential for Recovery Night. You may begin with a single group that includes everyone. At some point you may see a need to create groups that address the specific needs of teen addicts, sex/porn addiction, or family groups. Each one of these groups will need someone who can relate to the attendees. The brave souls who attend will begin to share and grow together into a new person in Christ.

o   Marketing for your recovery ministry is essential. The usual methods of fliers and bulletin inserts are a first step. You might place such fliers in public places such as the local coffee shop, hospital, counselors' offices, or high school websites. If you have a website, make sure you list it as one of the options that your church is offering. A short video of someone inviting people to come can be highly effective.

o   Remember there is a need for the person to have the will to recover. The addict's ownership of the problem and intention to begin recovery has to come first. As a family or friend, your personal journey needs to be addressed by groups such as Al-Anon.

o   The addiction may be the result of an emotional wound or PTSD that may need to be addressed with long-term counseling.

Relevant Scripture Verses to Help You with the Care of the Addicted

o   Matthew 11:28-30 (NRSV)—"Come to me, all you that are weary and are carrying heavy burdens, and I will give you rest. Take my yoke upon you, and learn from me; for I am gentle and humble in heart, and you will find rest for your souls. For my yoke is easy, and my burden is light."

o   Romans 8:26, 37-38 (NRSV)—"Likewise the Spirit helps us in our weakness; for we do not know how to pray as we ought, but that very Spirit intercedes with sighs too deep for words. . . . In all these things we are more than conquerors through him who loved us."

o   Romans 7:15-20—These verses are impactful for those struggling with addiction while desiring to do good.

o   Romans 12:1—Offer your body as a living sacrifice.

o   Lamentations 3:40—Examine our ways and return to God's path for us.

o   James 4:10—Good will lift you up.

o   1 John 1:9—God will forgive us and purify us.

o   1 John 5:14-15—God hears us when we ask.

o   Philippians 3:12-16—Forget what is behind and press forward.

Suggested Reading

o   *Addict in the Family: Stories of Loss, Hope and Recovery* by Beverly Conyers

o   *Codependent No More: How to Stop Controlling Others and Start Caring for Yourself* by Melody Beattie

o   *The Alcoholics Anonymous Big Book* by AA Services

Melissa's Sidebar

On September 30, 2019, I got the call I'd been dreading for fifteen years. "Melissa, it's Mama. Brandon—he didn't make it this time." The room spun as I fell down in shock, mouth open, and I started dry heaving as the news set in. My brother had died of an overdose. For seventeen long years he struggled with the disease of addiction that started with a sports injury and too many prescription pills.

Cut to three months later when I received an email from a fellow pastor in town. A "generous" family had decided to bestow the Christmas gift of heat to one lucky family, no strings attached! The email went on to say that they wanted to make sure that they were paying for someone's bills who actually deserved it—you know, not a drinker, smoker, or druggie.

My grief turned to rage. Brandon would have deserved heat in the bleak midwinter, regardless of whether or not he was using at the time, and I still can't get over the flippant way this pastor called folks who have the disease of addiction "druggies." Pastors: language matters. When we use words like that to describe an actual human being made in the image of God, we reduce a person to their struggle. Brandon was so much more than his struggle. He was sweet, playful, and full of pranks. His sense of humor, laughter, and smile were infectious, and everyone who knew him loved him. He was kind of shy but would fill the silence with an unexpected zinger that made everyone in the room laugh. Brandon spent hours every day playing in the woods as a boy; and as he grew, he came to love fishing out on our great-grandparents' land. On rainy days, when we couldn't play outside, we would find him constructing elaborate forts out of pillows, blankets, string, and any other household items he could find. He loved going to the lake, especially around the Fourth of July, where he would spend the whole day popping fireworks with friends and family. Brandon was a history buff, skilled welder, and an artist at heart. But no one who saw him on the side of the road begging would ever know that, and it pains me to say that very few, if any, churches in my hometown knew his gifts. Many knew his struggle. Ministry leaders, I beg you to have compassion and mercy on the millions of people struggling with addictions of all sorts.

For each person struggling with addiction, there is also a web of people additionally affected by it. I urge you to consider care ministry for friends and family of loved ones who may have lost their lives, continue to struggle, or remain alienated. Often, family members must define very difficult boundaries with their loved ones in order to remain healthy and whole, while not enabling destructive behavior. Sometimes, family cannot be family, no matter how much we want to. In these cases, I dream of a world in which the church can be the surrogate family to those struggling with addiction.

Chapter Sixteen

Communal Trauma

All who believed were together and had all things in common; they would sell their possessions and goods and distribute the proceeds to all, as any had need.

—Acts 2:44-45 (NRSV)

Since the beginning of the church, Christians have recognized the need to care for one another to "all, as any had need." How we extend care during a natural disaster, a pandemic, post–mass shootings, or a financial disaster must be considered a team effort. That team is most effective when it involves the whole community and perhaps even extends out into a state or national effort.

As I (Karen) write this, we are in the tenth week of social distancing because of COVID-19, the first major global pandemic for the world since 1918. As the churches have locally addressed the needs of their people and the national church bodies have responded, there is much to consider. Humanity has been thrust into change that has happened sometimes by the hour.

No matter what type of communal disaster, there are some fundamental, creative ways that the church can immediately respond. For our purposes we will divide our response into three categories:

o   immediate response within the first twenty-four hours,

o   possible responses through the trauma, and

o   long-term changes.

Immediate Responses

Whether it be a natural disaster such as a hurricane, tornado, flooding, earthquake, or large-scale fires, *the key to all of this is the way we as the shepherds respond immediately.* The same holds true for pandemics, shootings, financial disaster, and national disaster.

As a child in our small country church, I can remember the response of the church after a major storm came through with hail and tornado touchdowns that decimated our crops and our farm in particular. I remember the pastor and other volunteers immediately calling on us and offering help with cleanup, meals, and emotional support. Over the years, our farm, along with others, suffered through years of drought, more hailstorms, and bankruptcies. What do the people need in such times?

o   Again, it may seem obvious, but call or go immediately to the scene if possible. In situations such as a pandemic your phone call may be the only way you have to respond. You are a first responder as a pastor and CCM. You represent the presence of Christ.

o   Listen to the stories of how people experienced the acute situation. Allow them to express their emotions. If they need a shoulder to cry on, be there for them. These are our people and to help them through their grief, pain, and fear is absolutely a place where the church can offer the light and hope of Christ.

o   Attend to any obvious physical needs such as water, food, hygiene, and sheltering needs.

o   Offer a very brief word of scripture (this is not the time to preach) and let them know you will be there with them as they go through this situation.

o   Pray for their comfort, strength, assurance, and peace.

o Before you leave or hang up, let them know how the church will be responding to them the next day or throughout.

On a Palm Sunday, some of our church members suffered from a hate crime shooting. Two of us were at the hospital immediately to offer care. Upon leaving the hospital, we were able to offer next steps of gathering at the affected family's home later that evening with anyone else that they'd like to invite. That evening, they had invited their closest friends to also give them support. Our teamwork began to expand as we considered their needs throughout the week and months ahead. The main family members were connected with at least one CCM who could connect with them specifically throughout the week.

Because of the situation, the team realized that there was underlying racism and political divides that were surfacing. The challenges of white supremacy, gun control, and discrimination were some of the issues.

Moving through the Trauma

Within twenty-four hours the church's strategy will begin to emerge. Remember: it is not the job of the people living through the crisis to call the church and ask for help. If you wait for people to ask it is a formula for failure. As a church we must be the ones reaching out. You may try some things that may not work and that is OK. Keep being creative as a team for whatever you think is needed.

Remember how Jesus kept asking Peter in John 21 the same question, "Do you love me?" And Peter would respond, "You know I do, Lord." And Christ would remind him, "Then feed my lambs" or "Take care of my lambs." As an individual, family, community, or nation moves through a trauma the church needs to be nimble, ready to adapt to a changing situation. Items to consider:

o Monitor and abide by local, state, and national guidelines. Look to your denominational leaders for resources, financial assistance, and first responders.

o   Communicate to your congregation so they understand why certain decisions are being made. Pastors and CCMs should be checking in regularly so that they communicate the same message to the congregation.

o   Ongoing fear, anxiety, grief, and financial need can be addressed with regular check-ins from pastors and CCMs. Depending on the congregation, the church community may expect the pastor to begin this process, but it is the work of the team to be able to multiply the support efforts.

o   Create trauma therapy programs, collaborating with mental health professionals so that both emotional and spiritual care can be conjoined for the recovery of both individuals and families, as well as communities. Many times, people are hesitant to reach out for mental health care. At moments when there is communal trauma the church may offer an initial pathway for people to move past their shame or stigmas about obtaining mental health care.

o   Weekly worship is one way to name and remember how God is faithful through pain and disasters. As emphasized previously, an understanding of how God works in the world is so important. God gives us the great gift of choice and has set in place a world that may experience natural disasters. Thus people have found themselves on a beach when a tsunami has occurred. God allowed them the choice to go to the beach. Then the earthquake occurred in the ocean, which caused the tsunami. Emphasize that God walks alongside us no matter what happens. God weeps with us during these challenging situations.

o   A sermon series or at least one sermon to address the situation should be considered. People may need to think through the big "Why?" question, or consider how Christian hope extends beyond the current situation.

o   Care classes or groups may need to be created. In the case of a pandemic or financial crisis there may be a need for different varieties of prayer and meditation classes. Are there ways to help people with their job searches in the middle of a financial crisis?

o   Is there a need for food and water (both immediately and ongoing)? Open your church and your kitchen to organize the ongoing need.

o   If there is a need for immediate funerals, guide the family(s) and work as a team. During the pandemic, when funerals have not been happening in the usual way, be creative. Some churches provided Zoom or Facebook Live services while following social distancing rules. If a graveside service is allowed, other support can be experienced as congregants drive by or sit in the parking lot in their cars.

o   In some situations, a celebration of life can be planned with the person who is terminal and can actually be provided before the person dies. If there can be no service in the sanctuary, create other ways to celebrate such as through a Zoom service.

o   Utilize existing volunteers to provide for new needs such as facemasks (pandemic), sandbags (flooding), or volunteer construction crews.

Long-Term Changes

During and after any major disaster, the church will want to evaluate how they responded and if there might be any long-term changes that may be needed. The evaluation questions might include:

o   How do you offer worship?

o   How was follow-up created?

o   How was spiritual and emotional care offered?

o   How was financial care boosted?

o   How was safe housing provided?

o   How was educational help provided?

o   How were collaborative efforts offered and received?

o   How was food insecurity addressed?

During a time of disaster, a church who tries to work alone will have less impact than a group of churches or community organizations. Collaboration and team-building skills are key to the recovery of a community.

It probably states the obvious, but when a church runs toward a communal disaster and offers Christlike care, it can be an amazing time of building the church as we walk beside all of those who are in need. Answering Christ's call to "feed his lambs" can help us become the church of the future.

Questions to Consider

1. What has your church learned through any communal challenges?

2. Are you prepared for communal disasters?

3. How can your denomination help?

4. Are you establishing collaborative work throughout your community?

Acknowledgments

This book is the result of the cooperative efforts of many people over a decade of practicing care in churches throughout the United States. A multitude of pastors and CCMs have given their time, expertise, and wisdom as they have shared their stories to help the technical logistics come alive.

Special thanks go to leaders throughout the country who have given insight regarding organizing the CCM method of care in different-size churches. Rev. Laura Berg (New Smyrna Beach, FL) and Rev. Joy Dister-Dominquez (Fort Worth, TX) were especially helpful in developing case studies and organizational techniques.

Others who contributed were James Cochran, MA, LCPC, NCC; Pastor Tom Langhofer (currently serving as recovery pastor at the United Methodist Church of the Resurrection); and Rev. Bill Gepford (UMC pastor). Special thanks go to the congregational care ministries and the communication ministry at the United Methodist Church of the Resurrection who helped make this work accessible.

This book was published by Abingdon Press. Constance Stella, our editor, has been invaluable in her guidance and belief in the project!

Lastly, we want to thank our spouses, Les Lampe and Bill Gepford, who have supported our efforts with the understanding that the care ministries are essential to providing the heart to any church.

Notes

1. First Essential: Recruit and Equip

1. The Apostolic Constitutions 19.

2. Cyprian of Carthage, Letters 56:5.

3. Lampe, Karen, *The Caring Congregation Training Manual and Resource Guide* (Nashville: Abingdon Press, 2014), 27.

10. Visitation

1. *The United Methodist Book of Worship* (Nashville: The United Methodist Publishing House, 1992), 614.

14. Mental Health Ministry

1. *The Book of Discipline of The United Methodist Church* (Nashville: The United Methodist Publishing House, 2016), par. 161.

15. Recovery Ministry

1. 2016 Surgeon General Report on Alcohol, Drugs and Health.

Made in the USA
Columbia, SC
16 February 2024

31888464R00113